Lead. Care. Win.

DAN PONTEFRACT

Lead
Care
Win

How to Become a Leader Who Matters

Figure.1

Copyright © 2020 by Dan Pontefract

21 22 23 24 5 4 3 2

Cataloguing data are available from Library and Archives Canada

ISBN 978-1-77327-132-3 (pbk.)
ISBN 978-1-77327-133-0 (ebook)
ISBN 978-1-77327-134-7 (pdf)
ISBN 978-1-77327-135-4 (audio)

Design by Jessica Sullivan
Author photograph by Nadya Glouchak

Editing by Don Loney
Copy editing by Peter Norman

Printed and bound in Canada by Friesens
Distributed internationally by Publishers Group West

Figure 1 Publishing Inc.
Vancouver BC Canada
www.figure1publishing.com

To you, the reader.
Thank you for caring.
Si vis amari, ama.

Contents

Heroism

It takes great strength to train
To modern service your ancestral brain;
To lift the weight of the unnumbered years
Of dead men's habits, methods, and ideas;
To hold that back with one hand, and support
With the other the weak steps of a new thought.
It takes great strength to bring your life up square
With your accepted thought, and hold it there;
Resisting the inertia that drags back
From new attempts to the old habit's track.
It is so easy to drift back, to sink;
So hard to live abreast of what you think!
It takes great strength to live where you belong
When other people think that you are wrong;
People you love, and who love you, and whose
Approval is a pleasure you would choose.
To bear this pressure and succeed at length
In living your belief—well, it takes strength.
And courage too. But what does courage mean
Save strength to help you face a pain foreseen?
Courage to undertake this lifelong strain
Of setting yours against your grandsire's brain;
Dangerous risk of walking lone and free
Out of the easy paths that used to be,
And the fierce pain of hurting those we love
When love meets truth, and truth must ride above?

But the best courage man has ever shown
Is daring to cut loose and think alone.
Dark as the unlit chambers of clear space
Where light shines back from no reflecting face.
Our sun's wide glare, our heaven's shining blue,
We owe to fog and dust they fumble through;
And our rich wisdom that we treasure so
Shines from the thousand things that we don't know.
But to think new—it takes a courage grim
As led Columbus over the world's rim.
To think it cost some courage. And to go—
Try it. It taxes every power you know.
It takes great love to stir a human heart
To live beyond the others and apart.
A love that is not shallow, is not small,
Is not for one, or two, but for them all.
Love that can wound love, for its higher need;
Love that can leave love though the heart may bleed;
Love that can lose love; family, and friend;
Yet steadfastly live, loving, to the end.
A love that asks no answer, that can live
Moved by one burning, deathless force—to give.
Love, strength, and courage. Courage, strength, and love,
The heroes of all time are built thereof.

CHARLOTTE PERKINS GILMAN, 1898

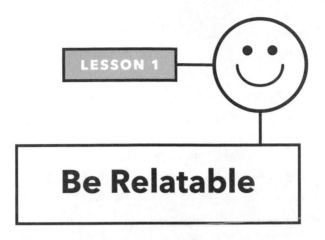

Be Relatable

LOOK AROUND. What do you see?

If you're like me, you see a world desperately in need of your help. It matters not if it's at work, home, on holiday or at the park. People everywhere—across all walks of life—are yearning for a stronger form of humanity to step forward. The SARS-CoV-2 (coronavirus) pandemic of 2020 clearly illustrated this need. How we care about and treat others is in need of an inquest.

Now ask yourself this question. When was the last time you had an honest exchange with another person, one that was so moving it might have even changed your life (let alone theirs)? Throughout the following pages we are going to talk about this great divide, outlining how and why it happens in the workplace and elsewhere. The problems are candid, but the corrective lessons are succinct and easily applied.

While we often hear the mantra that leaders are in the people business, something continues to be lost in translation. Let me make it clear: you are in the *relationship* business. Your number one and irrefutable goal is to focus your leadership on the development and sustainability of relationships. They could be with your family, neighbors, team members, bosses, partners, customers, suppliers or even competitors. The entirety of *Lead. Care. Win.* focuses on your exchanges with people and how to make them more meaningful and mutually productive.

The first lesson in this book centers on relatability. Just how relatable you are in all of your relationships—be they at work or outside of it—is a hallmark of leadership. I went looking for a story to help introduce the concept in this opening lesson. That story came to me on the day I was delivering a live webinar to an audience during the spring of 2019. In the middle of the session it serendipitously dawned on me: "How the heck did Zoom get to be so popular and why do so many people love it?"

Zoom is an online collaboration tool that allows you to host video meetings and conversations from any device. It was founded in 2011. Zoom was the service I used during that webinar session. By the time the pandemic hit, the use of Zoom skyrocketed from ten million daily users to well over two hundred million. The tool includes chat systems, screen sharing, document exchange, and a host of other features. On April 18, 2019, the company went public on NASDAQ and was valued at just under $16 billion by the end of its IPO. As of this writing it's up well over 200 percent with a market capitalization greater than $50 billion.

The last thing I wanted to do in a book about a more caring form of leadership was to highlight another high-tech company from Silicon Valley. Many stories from that part of the world are not to my liking. But as I researched Zoom to quench my curiosity,

I became much intrigued. I reached out to its founder, Eric Yuan. He responded the very day I sent him an introduction and said yes to my request for an interview. Naturally, we used Zoom.

"Dan, we are here to make people's lives better. Love is everything. If you truly love a customer or employee or partner, you will do whatever you can for them." These were not the first words I was expecting to hear from the founder and CEO of an online collaboration tool based in Silicon Valley. But they were powerful words, and a clear example of Yuan's view that the more relatable you are, the better things will be. It was a perfect start to a conversation about leadership.

His energy and passion regarding relationships shot through his office webcam, so much so I thought I was face to face with him for the duration of our time together. "When I was a kid, I never thought about it," he said. "I was taught to be very kind to people by my parents. Now, at Zoom, we know that if an employee is not happy, the customer will not be happy. It's all about relationships."

Happiness, love and looking out for others are key traits to Yuan's relatability style. Evidently it's working. Customer satisfaction is off the charts.[1] The company's net promoter score—a loyalty metric that measures a customer's willingness to return for another purchase and likelihood of recommending the company to family, friends or colleagues—is 62. Scores higher than zero are typically considered to be good, while scores above 50 are excellent. Anything below zero is a negative experience. For comparison, eBay's NPS score is 9, Costco's is 79 and Facebook's is pegged at minus 21.

Not everything has been rosy. During the pandemic, Zoom came under public fire for several security and privacy issues, particularly related to its Free Basic and Single Pro licenses. Zoom was originally intended to be an enterprise customer product, but with so many organizations switching to online meetings and classroom learning via Zoom, issues began to crop up. For example, some malevolent users began "Zoombombing," disrupting Zoom meetings uninvited and sharing shocking or even pornographic content due to a lack of passwords and easy access to the Zoom rooms. Yuan quickly stepped up, accepting blame, apologizing and immediately committing to fix any of the issues. In a blog post in early April, 2020, Yuan wrote:

> Transparency has always been a core part of our culture. I am committed to being open and honest with you about areas where we are strengthening our platform and areas where users can take steps of their own to best use and protect themselves on the platform.
>
> We welcome your continued questions and encourage you to provide us with feedback - our chief concern, now and always, is making users happy and ensuring that the safety, privacy, and security of our platform is worthy of the trust you all have put in us.[2]

It's what a caring leader ought to do in any sort of crisis. Be open and transparent, and look out for those you serve. It's the very definition of being relatable.

But how did Zoom come to be? Why did it become so popular? And why are its two thousand employees so happy at work?

After emigrating from China, Yuan joined an antecedent to Zoom in 1997 as a young engineer. The company name was Webex.

During the dot-com bubble mania, the company went public. A few years later, it was acquired by telecommunications giant Cisco for $3.2 billion. By 2010, Yuan questioned his happiness. Cisco was unwilling to invest in a complete rebuild in Webex, something Yuan was pushing for. He saw how slow and unfriendly the Webex experience had become for users. He no longer felt he was relating to the customers, let alone the company he worked for. Yuan was in charge of eight hundred engineers. What to do?

According to Yuan, Cisco didn't care about the customer's video conferencing experience. It wasn't interested in relating to the customer's needs. Cisco was more focused on building an enterprise version of Facebook. Further, the culture at Cisco had become too much for Yuan. "Every day, I was going into the office and I was very unhappy," he said. "And so were my customers. It was a negative impact to me and everyone." Yuan left in 2011 and immediately started work on Zoom. The rest, as they say, is history.

"Our company has a culture of delivering happiness," Yuan said. "Our company values are but one word: care. We care about each other, our customers, the community, Zoom, and ourselves. If you don't care, then you come across as always being right. And I'm not always right. Be humble, admit mistakes. And don't be so arrogant. We're only human."

I could have chatted with Eric Yuan for hours. A mere sixty minutes, however, provided rare insights into someone who believes that if you are relatable, everyone can win. He may be a multi-billionaire—and operating out of Silicon Valley—but Yuan built his successful career by caring, admitting mistakes and acting with humility, all the while looking out for others throughout the journey. In a nutshell, lead, care, and then you will win.

The Problem

New York Times columnist Paul Krugman once suggested that the United States is a nation suffering from an "epidemic of infallibility."[3] I share his sentiment, to a point. It's not just infallibility, and it's not a malady exclusive to America. It's our misunderstanding of the importance of relatability. We may think we're infallible, but that often boils down to our unwillingness to accept that we make mistakes and that we need help. Positioning ourselves as infallible is the antithesis of being relatable. Further, when we don't care about how others feel, people see right through us.

The problem comes down to this: we resist acknowledging we are fallible and imperfect. In his 1711 poem "An Essay on Criticism: Part 2," Alexander Pope wrote: "To err is human; to forgive, divine."[4] We recognize the idiom these days as "To err is human." But Pope had it right with the full line.

We have an ingrained cognitive dissonance—a formidable belief that we are fair, kind and unfailing and so perfectly relatable—yet we can easily fall into the trap of acting in ways that are far from benevolent. We of course do not see this blind spot—we deny it, insisting to ourselves "it's the other person." The cognitive dissonance that we suffer from runs counter to Pope's benediction for humanity. To be relatable, we need to appreciate that we make mistakes. Thus, to err is part of our DNA. Thinking you are infallible becomes the quickest path to coming off as a know-it-all. Do you really want to be thought of by others as that person who thinks they understand everything, who never makes a mistake and is intolerant of any human slip? That's not only utterly unkind, it is antithetical to a caring form of leadership.

Part of the problem rests with our inability to accept that we will indeed make mistakes: big ones, little ones and daily ones. Get over it. Eric Yuan makes them—and made them during the pandemic—but he's able to do so knowing it's his sincerity that pushes others to help him fix them. Further, when we feel as though we're not allowed to make mistakes at work, there's no hope for forgiveness because that's not part of the equation either. Thus we fail to forgive. Leadership without relatability results in a spiral of inhumaneness, a conspicuous lack of emotional intelligence.

To become relatable—to be a beacon of forgiveness and kindness, to be humble enough to ask for help—affects the very heart of your leadership. Caring for and about others means acknowledging your humanity and avoiding falling into the cognitive dissonance trap, which will cripple your ability to be relatable, and will consequently impact your team and what this group of good people are hopeful of achieving on your behalf.

5 LEADERSHIP QUESTIONS TO ASK YOURSELF:

1. Do I exhibit behaviors where I come across as an uncaring person?
2. Do I pretend to be someone I'm not?
3. Do I understand the impact of being disconnected from my work and my team?
4. Have I invested time in getting to know others as human beings?
5. When I make a mistake, do I ignore it, cover it up, or place blame elsewhere?

Why Relatability Matters

The first thing to get torched when you do not relate well to others is your reputation. (Signs that your reputation may need to be salvaged are given below.) You can be assured no one will be saying nice things about you if you continually behave in a manner that suggests you are better than others, pretending you are infallible. Instead, your reputation—your very identity—will be laid to waste. There isn't a hazmat suit in the world that will save you.

Are you confused as to why people are not sharing information with you? Ask yourself if you've burned bridges by being unkind to your peers. When was the last time you apologized for a mistake you inadvertently or blatantly made? If you cannot ask for help—or be proactive in the giving of assistance—you offer no inducement to others to want to forgive your selfishness. The corollary is an unflattering reputation. No one wants to be in your corner. Your network? In shambles.

The effect can end up becoming a grocery list of harmful ingredients. Not only will people be unwilling to share, but they will also refrain from advocating for you when it comes time for project selections, promotions, development opportunities or even social activities.

You also invite employee apathy. We need more empathy, not apathy. If team members see you acting in such an unthoughtful manner, their willingness to go above and beyond the call of duty or to provide you with assistance becomes near impossible. "Why exert any extra effort at all," some will say, "if my leader is grossly aloof and uncaring and never admits to a mistake? It's impossible to relate to this person. I give up."

When apathy takes hold, productivity wanes, engagement drops, and whatever the team is tasked to accomplish becomes less of a priority. There is no doubt that employees will soon say, "What's the point?" This terrible indifference is the consequence of those who lead without caring, fail to be relatable and even lack the decorum to say "bless you" after someone sneezes.

YOUR "RELATABILITY QUOTIENT" IS IN PERIL WHEN:

You equate leadership with unwavering toughness.

You operate with two personalities: one for work and one for outside of work. (How will people know the "real" you?)

You refuse to ask sincere questions about the well-being of team members.

You do not bother to inspire the team because you view it as a waste of time.

You believe errors are intolerable and saying sorry doesn't make up for stupidity.

You never make a mistake, and have convinced yourself of such tragic nonsense.

Go to www.LeadCareWin.com/scorecard *and assess your Be Relatable score. It will only take a couple of minutes. Then return to the book.*

Ideas for Becoming More Relatable

You can become more relatable by kick-starting six relationship-building leadership habits. They are:

▶ RESPECT OTHERS

▶ EMPATHIZE

▶ BE PERSONABLE

▶ MANAGE MISTAKES

▶ APOLOGIZE

▶ ASK FOR HELP AND FEEDBACK

▶ RESPECT OTHERS

Being relatable is rooted in civility. If your default position is to respect others, there is a far greater chance of your relationships blossoming. After all, it's how *we* want to be treated. Consider these aspects of respecting others:

Be patient with a request you've made, yet be proactive when following up:
· Don't badger someone to death if they haven't answered your query. Employ tolerance.
· Don't be so reactive that there isn't sufficient time for someone to respond. Act with composure.

Genuinely care in all of your interactions:
· Don't aggressively and madly bark orders, demands or asks. Invoke calmness.
· Don't be impolite to the point of forgetting how to be civil with others. Act with courtesy.

Be positive and thoughtful in written correspondence and verbal exchanges:

· Don't use negative, hostile or impolite language in texts, emails, instant messages, etc. Consider graciousness.
· Don't be passive-aggressive, hurtful or demeaning when face to face. Employ positivity.

Use friendly, helpful gestures in all of your exchanges:
· Don't cut someone off, slam a door in their face or fail to say hello in an elevator. Use good manners.
· Don't ignore their requests, purposely delete their texts/emails or fail to lend a hand. Act cooperatively.

America's first female self-made millionaire, Sarah Breed-love—known as Madame C.J. Walker—was an African-American entrepreneur in the late 1800s and early 1900s. She pioneered the development and marketing of hair care products and cosmetics. As a profitable entrepreneur, Breedlove could have overlooked the needs of her employees. Instead, she respected their thoughts and hunger for growth. Her business employed well over three thousand workers in the US, and a large portion of those were door-to-door saleswomen. She was known to be overly generous, getting to know many of her employees through the in-depth training sessions she delivered. In 1912, Breedlove said, "Now my object in life is not simply to make money for myself or to spend it on myself in dressing or running around in an automobile, but I love to use a part of what I make to help others."[5] Breedlove was a leader who respected the needs of those who worked for her. In sum, she cared.

▶ EMPATHIZE

Empathy is a multi-faceted concept. At its root is your ability to proactively—and sometimes reactively—consider the emotional feelings and intellectual thoughts of the other person. I have witnessed empathy, when used correctly, become a highly influential tactic through a three-fold process:

· Head
· Heart
· Hands

When you appreciate how someone thinks—how they are mentally processing a situation—you are demonstrating what psychologists refer to as *cognitive empathy*. You are using your head to get inside their head. This is about how they think. They're likely looking at the world through a different lens than yours. Perhaps it's their politics, religion, upbringing, culture, sexuality, language, ethnicity or something else. Whatever the case, if you appreciate where people are coming from conceptually, you demonstrate empathy with your head.

When you try to understand how the other person is feeling, you are using your heart to get inside their heart. Psychologists call this *emotional empathy*. It's about how people sense situations. Perhaps those you are trying to relate to are sensitive to or get deeply emotional in certain scenarios. Maybe there is a concern for animals, or children, or the underprivileged, or the environment. Maybe they're simply having a bad day at work and feeling a bit off. Whatever the cause, if you arrive at understanding how people are emotionally feeling in specific situations, you demonstrate empathy with your heart.

When you are able to relate to how someone is thinking *and* feeling, your hands are now in play. Metaphorically, you are using your hands to take action, to address the situation with something known as *sympathetic empathy*. Once you have satisfactorily assessed or interpreted the other person's head and heart—where they are coming from cognitively and emotionally—you are in a better position to do something about it. It's how you can turn empathy into positive action.

When you understand and employ all three categories of empathy—head, heart and hands—you have given birth to compassion. Compassion is thus the offspring of empathy. It is a critical piece to a high-functioning and caring relationship. A compassionate person is one who relates with others and employs all three types of empathy.

Contemplate these strategies in your quest to be more relatable through the three types of empathy:

Not all is as it seems, so give the other person the benefit of the doubt:
- Don't think for a second everything is peachy in the other person's world. They come to work with real problems at home, too.
- Don't expect someone's personal life to be left at the door. Their feelings often have no barrier.

Everyone has an opinion and position on things, and they're likely to be different than yours:
- Don't disregard someone's background, ethnicity, religion, history or politics. They need you to appreciate their differences.

· Don't overlook their professional background or past roles. They have biases and strengths that might alter your thinking.

Remember how it feels to be treated like gold by someone else. Now do that for others:

· Don't overlook the state of mind and emotion of others. They need your warmth.
· Don't overestimate the pure brilliance of asking how someone else is feeling. They need your caring.

▶ BE PERSONABLE

To be relatable is to portray yourself as a real human being. If your only point of reference in life is your current role and place of work, people will view you as being impersonal. When you bring your whole self to work, you look to share some of your more personal details when pertinent. Consider these ideas:

Share your personality

Where do you come from? What was your upbringing? Who were your favorite role models? Did you have any struggles growing up? Do you like butterscotch ice cream? What current hobbies do you enjoy? Are you heading to a Billie Eilish concert soon? What about an upcoming holiday plan? What did you do to stay motivated during the pandemic when being quarantined at home? Team members and colleagues appreciate it when someone is willing to share parts of their real selves outside of work. It makes you relatable to others. For example, I love interior design and decorating. I'm also afraid of heights. Now you know.

Share your career stories

Similar to sharing your personality, when you reflect back and draw upon and share the ocean of experience that you have likely acquired in other roles or organizations, it demonstrates your willingness to give back, to impart wisdom. In parallel, you are opening yourself up through those stories to be viewed as a real person. Did you have a caring manager who became a mentor? What can you pay forward? In your experience, what organizations stand out as role models with values and habits you admire that deserve to be broadcast? These stories open the door to engaging others in a personable way. For example, my time at high-tech company Crystal Decisions, and the work of Tracy Logan, Alison Dawn Lee and Patricia Bjerrisgaard, taught me the significance of purpose and the critical importance of community giving. It informed much of my thinking on the matter for years to come.

▶ MANAGE MISTAKES

Msitakes happen. Yes, I just made one. Will the editors let it pass? Mistakes (or msitakes) are a part of us, whether we like it or not. Recall the idiom from earlier in the chapter: "To err is human." The unwillingness to recognize mistakes or ignore them altogether will hamper your efforts to relate to others. We must understand that a) every one of us makes mistakes, and b) there really are only two types of mistakes.

The first type, *simple mistakes*, are those that are relatively straightforward and can be remedied quickly. For example, you didn't respond to an email because you were "busy." Maybe you forgot to thank someone for their hard work. Did you forget to attend that coffee catch-up meeting? Making simple mistakes is part of life. Ignoring them or trying to cover the mistakes up doesn't improve your relatability, and in fact it can hamper it.

Complex mistakes are a result of poor planning, decision-making and thinking. Their complexity may not be solely your fault, but somehow you are involved and they're mistakes nonetheless. In 2018, KFC restaurants across the UK fell into supply chain issues and ran out of chicken, forcing the company to temporarily close nearly six hundred of its nine hundred stores. You can imagine the leadership headaches that were transpiring at the time. How could a chicken restaurant run out of its main ingredient, chicken!?! It was a complex mistake between the company, suppliers and delivery companies, one where thousands of dollars were lost.

▶ **APOLOGIZE**

There is an argument to be made that we frequently make simple and complex mistakes. As we've learned, you might miss a text or instant message from someone. You forget to upload a file to the cloud drive that a colleague was waiting on. You are on your mobile phone going through a door, and you let the door slam in the face of the person behind you, oblivious that anyone was there until you hear, "Thanks a lot, jerk."

Thus, there are ample chances for you to apologize throughout a month. It's the very essence of being relatable to others. Saying sorry demonstrates a willingness to make a wrong known swiftly, and to take accountability for it. Eric Yuan immediately did so after the privacy and security issues of Zoom were made known during the pandemic.

Let's say you listened to a voicemail that was left by a colleague. It was of the urgent variety. You got distracted, deleted it by accident and then completely forgot to call back. You receive an email the next day from your teammate wondering why you didn't call back. It's the perfect time to say sorry, explain what happened, address the issue at hand and move on. Ignoring it or failing to say sorry only casts a negative shadow in your direction.

When a complex mistake is made, a more formal apology is likely necessary. In personal situations it could be a heart-to-heart chat, a card or even the offer of a bottle of wine.

In my homeland, Canada, the federal government formally apologized to those affected by heinous historical acts such as the country's appalling record on Indigenous residential schools, Japanese internment camps, the Chinese head tax and the turning away of Jewish refugees fleeing Nazism. It did so by issuing official statements in the House of Commons and tendering financial compensation. Those are formal apologies based on very complex mistakes.

When those KFC restaurants across the UK ran out of chicken, the company had to make amends for its complex mistake. It started on Twitter, with a short tweet trying to explain things: "The Chicken Crossed the Road, Just Not to Our Restaurants..." A formal apology was subsequently delivered to its customers via full-page newspaper adverts. The ad contained a chicken bucket with the KFC label cleverly changed to "FCK." The text below it read:

> We're Sorry. A chicken restaurant without any chicken. It's not ideal. Huge apologies to our customers, especially those who traveled out of their way to find we were closed. An endless

> thanks to our KFC team members and our franchise partners for working tirelessly to improve the situation. It's been a hell of a week, but we're making progress, and every day more and more fresh chicken is being delivered to our restaurants. Thank you for bearing with us.[6]

For both KFC and the Government of Canada, the formal apologies were also acts of relatability. Saying sorry is not admitting to a character flaw; it is a skillful demonstration of self-awareness. When it's timely and genuine, even better. Self-deprecation is also a wonderful ally, as was demonstrated at the chicken pen of Colonel Sanders.

▶ **ASK FOR HELP AND FEEDBACK**

You might possess a natural reluctance to ask for assistance. It doesn't feel right. We question our competence or how we might be perceived by others. "If I ask for help, won't I look dumb or weak?"

To relate to others, you have to get over the discomfort of requesting help. Asking for help or feedback is not a condemnation of your aptitude; it is a sign of respect.

In fact, research suggests that we underestimate by as much as 50 percent the likelihood that others would agree to our requests.[7] Put simply, your colleagues are more willing to provide support than you believe to be the case. So the first bubble to burst is about the claim itself. You won't come off as looking inept when asking for help or feedback. And when you ask, people view you more humanly, another step towards relatability.

There are four types of requests for help or feedback we can initiate. They are:

1. Personal
Individual needs to help you get unblocked. Examples: missing details on a large-scale org change, feedback on a personality issue or coaching support after someone is terminated.

2. Project-based
Assistance with assignments and tasks. Examples: missing data, information or knowledge for a project to proceed or the need to be introduced to someone to move a project along.

3. Managerial
Requests made to your direct manager. Examples: career development asks, performance coaching requests or budgetary needs.

4. Team-based
Asking the team for assistance. Examples: 360-degree feedback opportunities or workload imbalance discussions.

Asking for help or feedback is not a weakness. It is the epitome of being honest with your fallibility. It is an example of leadership through vulnerability.

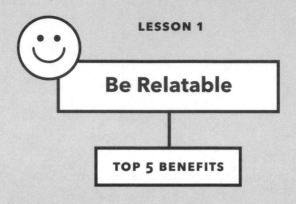

Be Relatable

TOP 5 BENEFITS

1. Your reputation will expand positively; others will want to work with you (and even for you).

2. It's very likely your role at work will feel more meaningful than just a job.

3. The ease with which you get things done will multiply by your increased level of relatability.

4. The chance for career progression or access to juicier projects will likely multiply.

5. You will be regarded as that person who genuinely cares about other people's feelings.

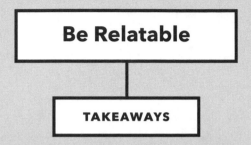

Be Relatable

TAKEAWAYS

Be more personal in your interactions with others. Be real. Open up. Show your underbelly.

Respect everyone you work with. Start by smiling, positively commenting on your colleague's efforts (e.g., "Excellent job!") and saying please and thank you.

Start taking ownership of your mistakes and apologize for them accordingly.

Empathize with others. Use your head, heart and hands to better appreciate peers and team members.

In summary, be relatable.

Visit www.LeadCareWin.com/extras *for recommended books, essays, videos, quotes, songs, poems and art related to Lesson 1: Be Relatable.*

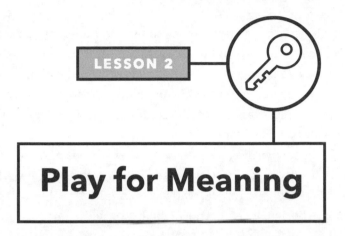

Play for Meaning

THE YEAR IS 1985, right around the time New Coke arrives in grocery stores, confusing millions of teenagers, including me. Mikhail Gorbachev is the leader of the Soviet Union. He's desperately trying not to be friends with Ronald Reagan. *Live Aid* rocks London and Philadelphia. Phil Collins plays in both locations, aided by the Concorde supersonic jet. Nintendo arrives into our living rooms along with its sensational hit *Super Mario Bros. Back to the Future* is crushing the box office. My hair is big. Very big. It's peak eighties.

In early 1985, fifty of America's most famous music artists are invited to meet in a secret location. It's a studio somewhere in Hollywood. There they will record an instant classic. It eventually goes on to become the fastest-selling American pop single in history. That year it also skyrockets to number one around the world. The song is "We Are the World." It sells over twenty million copies.

Activist and actor Harry Belafonte first came up with the idea. He was looking to respond to Bob Geldof's smash charity hit "Do They Know It's Christmas?" released in 1984 by acts based in the

United Kingdom. Belafonte aimed to support both African famine relief *and* America's own hunger crisis. Quincy Jones—the famous producer who happened to be involved with a little album called *Thriller*—gets involved. Several musicians are tasked with writing the song. The process eventually settles on two global megastars: Michael Jackson and Lionel Richie.

After a few writing sessions, the song's lyrics and melodies are finalized. Demo vocals are made and cassettes—yes, cassette tapes—are shipped to artists who have committed to the recording session. The date is set. It's now January 28, showtime.

The likes of Bob Dylan, Stevie Wonder, Cyndi Lauper, Dionne Warwick, Diana Ross, Billy Joel, Tina Turner and Bruce Springsteen arrive. It's late. Many were coming from the American Music Award ceremony, held that same night in Los Angeles. After their limousines drop them off at the studio—before they enter the hallowed halls of the A&M Recording Studios—the artists are met with a sign:

PLEASE CHECK YOUR EGOS AT THE DOOR.

The sign was the genius of Jones, the man producing the track. Why the sign?

Jones knew there might be trouble. It was a not-so-subtle reminder to the musicians that the song they were about to record wasn't about them. Heck, it wasn't *for* the artists either. They weren't singing to stroke their ego. It was about something more significant.

"We Are the World" was about singing for a higher purpose. It was an act of leadership not to fuel their own self-esteem or image but to help others, those in need.

Metaphorically, the musicians played not for the name on the back of their jersey but instead for the crest on the front. The crest might well have been a picture of humanity. The dilemma of whether to play for the front or the back is the ultimate character issue; it can be framed in the question "Why are we here?" It may be society's most existential question. (Sartre, anyone?) It's one of humanity's chief leadership problems.

Ask yourself, "Why am I here?" Many of us want the same things and have similar needs. A loving partner. Respect at work. The ability to feel valued, to contribute worth. Companionship, friendship and acceptance. Money to pay rent or the mortgage and take a vacation. A nice bottle of wine would be nice. Maybe a peppery Australian Shiraz. Good hair days.

How can we meet these needs and wants and aspire to great things yet be true to ourselves? How do you play? For your own gain or to see others through?

The Problem

The definition of hubris is as follows: "exaggerated pride or dangerous overconfidence." The definition of power—the non-electrical sort—is: "possession of control, authority or influence over others." Some people suffer from a self-indulgent, narcissistic arrogance. They then mix that with a toxic desperation to dominate. In the end, you have yourself a classic ego-driven leadership style. Is that you?

Think Donald Trump. It's low-hanging fruit, but bear with me and the plums we can easily pluck. He is the epitome of hubris and power. He plays solely for the name Trump—and his coterie—not for the whole that is America.

If you've ever read (or watched) *The Lord of the Rings*, you will be reminded of both hubris and power and how it can alter our behavior. Sméagol was once a joyful hobbit, but he eventually morphed into Gollum. Whereas previously he conducted himself with a sense of purpose, "the ring" corrupted his thinking. The quest for "the ring" became the singular goal akin to ruling over others. Gollum became what far too many people today mimic: he suffered from an addiction to self-centeredness assisted by an ego full of hubris aided by the quest for power. Too many people believe leadership is about reigning. Spoiler alert! Sméagol failed. (Actually, he died.)

Woven into your leadership fabric is the size of your ego. During an annual employee engagement survey, I worked with a leader who conducted a face-to-face meeting with his team, coercing them on how to score the results so he and the team would receive a high ranking. It was egregious and the epitome of selfish leadership. You may surmise correctly that not many people liked him, and you can be assured that his reputation was unfavorably lacquered by this quest for perfection.

Furthermore, the following year, when this particular leader received the results of his team's low engagement scores, he went on to blame them for their lack of engagement. Imagine faulting a team for not being engaged. Could it be the pot calling the kettle black? It was so absurd, I had to corroborate the feedback with some sleuth investigating. Unsurprisingly, not long after, he was fired.

When you're not checking your ego at the door as the "We Are the World" musicians did, you're not operating with meaning. You're not putting others ahead of your need for pomposity. You're in it for your version of "the ring," nothing more. You're using your ego to stamp out others in the path towards superiority. The goal is to win at whatever cost. That isn't operating bigger than your ego; it's working *to feed* your ego. And that's a problem.

5 LEADERSHIP QUESTIONS TO ASK YOURSELF

1. Do I understand why I am here?
2. Do I understand whom I am serving?
3. Do I understand what I am trying to accomplish in my role?
4. Do I understand where I can make the most impact?
5. Do I understand how I want others to think about me when I leave a room?

Why Playing for Meaning Matters

A focus on hubris and power will easily impede a more caring form of leadership. Whether they are peers, colleagues or team members you're leading, when you solely play for the sake of the name on the back of your jersey, people will question your values. (Signs that people are talking behind your back are given below.)

The consequence? Nobody wants to work *with* you or *for* you. Projects don't get done. Revenues suffer. That promotion you believe you deserve never materializes. Think of it as becoming the outcast at the high school dance, hanging by yourself in the corner wondering why everyone else is dancing.

Consider these two real-life examples with the names changed to protect the innocent.

Jane is a marketing director. Her forty-person team is made up of managers and their direct reports. Since becoming director a year or so ago, Jane has developed a tendency for taking personal credit for ideas that were the product of hard work by the team. Instead of promoting the team—and the ideas or accomplishments of those she was leading—she instead took credit for them. As the team learned about this, its engagement scores plummeted. Several people on the team ended up leaving the company. Others became checked out in their roles, refusing to initiate new ideas.

There is another example with a leader we'll call Pete. This interior designer runs a design firm of about ten people. One day at a meeting, while in front of a restaurant owner who had hired Pete and his team to remodel several establishments, Pete reprimanded his colleague Doug for not making design recommendations to the owner's liking. "I'm sorry for Doug's design options," said Pete to the restaurateur. "They're not up to my standards either, so shall we start over? I know what you're *really* looking for." With his skin tone turning bright red from utter embarrassment, Doug sheepishly apologized to the client. Wouldn't you know it though, a few days later, the client pulled the plug and went with a different interior design firm altogether. Doug was blamed for that, too.

When ego defines your leadership style, there are bound to be negative consequences.

YOUR "PLAY FOR MEANING" QUOTIENT MAY BE IN PERIL WHEN:

You care more about climbing the corporate ladder than using it to rescue a cat in a tree.

You come to work for the money, not the meaning.

You take credit for your team's work. (After all, you are the boss and your team wouldn't get things done without you.)

You make decisions based on what's in it for you, because you just know you deserve the money and kudos.

You believe your career comes first. Always.

You believe you hold the key to advancement of the team, so they must bend to your will.

Go to www.LeadCareWin.com/scorecard *and assess your Play for Meaning score. It will only take a couple of minutes. Then return to the book.*

Ideas for Operating with Meaning

Everyone needs a paycheck. Everyone has bills to pay. Everyone needs to eat. Narcissists aside, everyone wants (and needs) to be liked and loved. Holidays are a good thing. I love riding my bicycle across Tuscany. Each of us needs to ensure we are doing what we can to make enough money that satisfies our needs and at least a few of our wants. How do you achieve it?

If you want to improve how you lead self and others, you can begin by reflecting on the five questions posed above. Yes, they are existential in nature, but these questions center on purpose, a topic I covered in great detail in my second book, *The Purpose Effect*. I felt the need to revisit that book to determine if the overarching concept of purpose fit as a lesson of leadership. My analysis led to a resounding yes.

When we lead ourselves and others with a sense of purpose, we do so fully recognizing that there is more to this earth than just ego, money and power. The answers to the questions I posed may vary for you, but the following insights might help with your own journey as it relates to purpose.

▶ WHY AM I HERE?

If your goal is to make as much money or profit as possible, you really have to ask yourself, "What is the point?" Marc Benioff is the founder, CEO and chairman of high-tech company Salesforce. He echoes the sentiment. "Yes, profits are important, but so is society. And if our quest for greater profits leaves our world worse off than before, all we will have taught our children is the power of greed."[1] It turns out greed is *not* good.

Brian Scudamore, the founder of 1-800-GOT-JUNK, once said to me that his life's purpose is to make meaning, not money.[2] Brian's words have stuck with me ever since. Meaning is akin to purpose. When you recognize that you've only got one chance at life, the lens becomes crystal clear. Think Kobe Bryant. Before his tragic death he was just coming into his own, leading a reimagined life of higher purpose. Money, albeit important, does not create purpose. Meaning and purpose are established when you treat every situation as an opportunity to learn, to give, to understand, to create. When you remove hubris and power from your definition of leadership, you can begin to lead yourself and others with meaning:

Stop thinking that more money or profit (through increased power and hubris) are the only paths towards purpose.

Start your journey to meaning by creating a purpose statement that is expressive, relevant, and acts as a North Star for your daily interactions with others. Mine is as follows:

We're not here to see through each other;
We're here to see each other through.

▶ WHOM AM I SERVING?

This not a trick question. You possess a circle of influence. The problem is whether you are solely serving yourself or including those whom you have the fortune of influencing. It's not about forgoing personal development or advancing your career. It's whether or not your overall aims are selfish versus selfless. If a lifeguard only looks out for those they're interested in dating, that's a pretty selfish move. (It's somewhat unethical, too.) If a cyclist in the Tour de France never takes a turn at the front of a peloton to help create wind draft for others, that's another example of selfishness. If you symbolically kick people off the career ladder that you're trying to climb, it's another example of being egocentric.

If we pick favorites, we lose credibility. If we forget to involve key people in our decision-making or communication, we tarnish our name. When you serve others, you do so by simultaneously thinking of people's feelings, needs and wishes. As a leader, you must always remind yourself whom you are serving, taking steps to be inclusive and abundantly collaborative. In the end, nobody wants a leader who fails to be empathetic to the desires of others. Your aim is to serve all relevant stakeholders (team members, customers, society and the environment), not your ego. Let me be blunt:

· Stop blatantly ignoring the needs and feelings of those in your circle of influence;
· Start opening up your heart and mind to all stakeholders, treating them with your newly defined purpose.

Remind yourself that the more you are relatable and empathetic (as we learned from Lesson 1), the more likely it is that others become supportive of your own growth and development.

▶ WHAT AM I TRYING TO ACCOMPLISH, AND WHERE CAN I MAKE THE MOST IMPACT?

Famed monk and theologian Thomas Merton (a.k.a. Father Louis) once wrote: "If you want to identify me, ask me not where I live, or what I like to eat, or how I comb my hair, but ask me what I am living for, in detail, ask me what I think is keeping me from living fully for the thing I want to live for."[3]

You have a responsibility to think about and define what you are working towards and the impact you might make. A rudderless boat goes nowhere. A kite without wind remains grounded. A garden without water never grows. So, what are you trying to accomplish in your life, and what type of impact are you seeking to achieve? If those remain undefined—and ultimately not acted upon—you wind up living a life of ineffectiveness, let alone wasted opportunity.

If you are leading people, why not share your enthusiasm for leading, your aspirations for yourself and your wishes for the team? Michael Bungay Stanier, the founder of Box of Crayons and author of fantastic books such as *The Coaching Habit* and *The Advice Trap,* says to almost anyone that he meets that he's trying to "infect one billion people with the possibility virus."[4] I find that rather impressive. He's open, transparent, lofty and unafraid to wear his higher purpose ambitions on his sleeves for others to witness. (And he's definitely in it for meaning, not just money. His dress shirts are out of this world, too.) Consider these steps:

· Stop hiding behind an undefined development path or impact objective.
· Start by reflecting on what you want to achieve in the short term and long term with your working life.
· Next, write down your goals based on three criteria: work experiences, developmental and impact.
· Finally, define the changes you have to make in your life to reach those short- and long-term objectives.

Here's an example of the criteria mentioned above put into context. The number of items in each section can vary for you. Each term is intended to be viewed as "over the course of my career" statements.

Work experiences:
· I will work in the pharmaceutical, transportation and consumer goods industries.
· I will lead a team of up to one hundred people.

- I will work in a start-up as well as an organization with over $1 billion in revenues.
- I will work in a not-for-profit organization that helps underprivileged children.
- I will work in three different cities.

Developmental:
- I will achieve a Six Sigma Black Belt.
- I will deliver ten public talks at public conferences.
- I will contribute five editorial pieces to recognized magazines or online sites.
- I will receive a master's-level credential.

Impact:
- I will proactively offer to assist someone in my organization once per week.
- I will coach fifteen people to become leaders of people/teams.
- I will volunteer one thousand hours of community service.
- I will help the organizations I work for donate $1 million to those in need.
- I will make changes to diminish my personal CO_2 emissions.

Remember, for each of the three sections (work experiences, developmental and impact) you will also need to define the changes required to reach each of the objectives. (I've left that for you to handle.)

▶ HOW DO I WANT TO BE THOUGHT OF WHEN I LEAVE A ROOM?

For all his brilliant artistry and musicianship, there has been a question nagging me for many years when it comes to Prince. As a massive fan of his library, including such hits as "Raspberry Beret," "Pop Life" and "Sign o' the Times," I wonder why he didn't contribute to the recording of "We Are the World"? After all, he's Prince!

Before Quincy Jones's involvement, music producer Ken Kragen was tasked with sourcing musicians to play on the song. He reached out to Prince, who committed to being a part of the recording. At the last minute, he pulled out. Said Kragen, "One of the reasons Prince didn't turn up is because he always recorded alone and not with an engineer. All of a sudden, he couldn't be in a room with his peers. He knew it was a mistake. It was unfortunate that he didn't show."[5]

Prince never made it into the recording room that evening, but I have often wondered how much he regretted it. Did he think that his peers may have viewed him differently afterwards? Did they? Sadly, we'll never know. Thankfully he made up for it and recorded an entirely new song for inclusion on the *We Are the World* album, titled "4 the Tears in Your Eyes."

This story reminds us that every interaction we have with others is the opportunity to make an impression. Good or bad. And it also prompts us to ask the question, "How do you want to be known when you leave a room?" (Despite the irony of Prince never even making it *into* the recording room.)

Reputation is built one interaction at a time, often based on your values and sense of purpose. If you work with malice or forgetfulness or rudeness or disingenuousness or a quest for power, when you leave the room, you are regularly remembered for that and only that. It's a harsh reality, but it is also a clear line in the sand between caring and being a jerk.

STOP USING overconfidence and ego satisfaction as a basis for your daily interactions with others.

Start being polite, helpful, kind and sincere with every single interaction, even if you're feeling miserable, tired or moody.

Start remembering that the people you serve will only follow or look up to you if you relate with civility, purpose and mutual respect.

"In a sense, people are our proper occupation.... Our actions may be impeded by them, but there can be no impeding our intentions or our dispositions.... What stands in the way becomes the way."

■ **Marcus Aurelius**

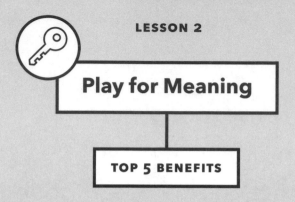

Play for Meaning

TOP 5 BENEFITS

1. Having meaning and purpose will make you happier instead of questing for power and ego satisfaction.

2. More people will want to work *with* and *for* you.

3. By looking out for others, you are far more likely to see opportunities boomerang back your way.

4. When things go sideways, people will give you the benefit of the doubt.

5. Nobody wants to end up like Sméagol—not even Sméagol.

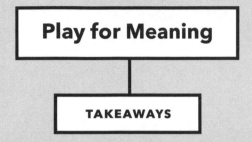

Play for Meaning

TAKEAWAYS

Begin to recognize that there is more to leadership than merely climbing a career ladder.

Draft a purpose statement that is meaningful and acts as a North Star for your interactions.

Be more empathetic and sympathetic to the feelings and ideals of peers versus solely your own needs and wants. (Continue to reflect on the empathy suggestions in Lesson 1: Be Relatable.)

Reflect on and decide your short-term and long-term working life achievements. Be specific. Write down those achievements based on three criteria: work experiences, developmental and impact. Capture the behavioral changes needed to accomplish each of them.

Stop solely playing for the name on the back of your jersey. Play for the crest on the front (all stakeholders).

Show up for your recording of "We Are the World" if asked.

Visit www.LeadCareWin.com/extras *for recommended books, essays, videos, quotes, songs, poems and art related to Lesson 2: Play for Meaning.*

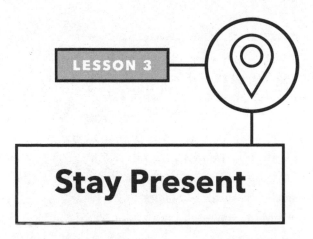

Stay Present

I MIGHT AS WELL have given this lesson the title *Time Is the Crime.*

Why? Most of us don't use our time very well. That in and of itself has become a crime. The systems we adopt to convince ourselves we are winning the time battle are mere illusion. The technology we use is a crutch. The apps are merely a Band-Aid. The New Year's resolutions become forgotten. To improve your ability to lead, you must come clean. Time is the enemy. And you're sleeping with the enemy every single day.

We feel chronically overwhelmed. "I'm just so busy," we say to anyone who dares to ask how we're doing. If you're hip, you call it "cray cray busy." Simultaneously, we're texting our boss. Our answer to the "How are you doing?" question is delivered with a lack of feeling usually reserved for epidurals. Ultimately our mismanagement of time has reached epic heights, the point at which it's detrimentally affecting our ability to lead self and others.

To counter the problem, we read a hopeful article about constructive use of time or attend a workshop on time management. We commit to change, but then fall back into the same time trap. Later we watch an inspiring TED Talk. It gives us a motivational jolt, but we remain blinded by the time light. We buy a fancy time management Moleskine. It sits on the shelf collecting dust next to your copy of *The 4-Hour Workweek*.[1] It's the term "time management" that produces a bitter irony. Time adultery, perhaps.

Whom should we look to blame?

In the United States, the Bureau of Labor Statistics indicates full-time employees work nearly nine hours a day.[2] The daily hours spent at work have been on the rise since the 1970s. What happened to the eight-hour workday, let alone the four-hour workweek? Like a sandcastle that got built when the tide was out, our intended structure is annihilated when the water comes in.

Worse, according to Glassdoor, full-time employees in the US take less than half of their allotted vacation time. On top of that, two-thirds of them admit to working while on holiday.[3] Commuting tells a story, too. In the US, commute times have risen from a one-way average of twenty-one minutes in 1980 to nearly twenty-seven minutes today.[4] That's nearly 30 percent higher. It's no better in Tokyo, where one-way commute times average forty-nine minutes.[5] Across the whole of Germany, it's sixty minutes.[6] Thus, commuting has become a global issue.

Time management isn't the answer, however. That type of thinking is a boatload of balderdash. You can't manage time, because time is a constant. There are 168 hours every week. Deal with it. Get over it. You can, however, manage your *behavior* as it relates to time. Behavior change is the key. Being in the moment, mindful and focused is critical to leading self and others. I call it the ability to *stay present*.

Which is why the story of Basecamp is so intriguing. Basecamp is an online project management tool. It originated out of necessity. In 1999, Jason Fried founded a web design company called 37signals. Realizing there was no useful web-based collaboration tool that allowed communication and project management to go hand in hand, he and his co-founder, David Heinemeier Hansson, developed Basecamp.

Jason and David invited customers to use the platform to collaborate on their projects. The customers loved the tool, perhaps even more than the company's web design services. By 2004, Basecamp became the product—as well as the company's name—and the rest is history. Goodbye managing projects by cumbersome "reply all" email chains. Hello Basecamp.

Since its inception the company has successfully gained over three million unique subscribers to the Basecamp platform. I'm one of them. It really is a fab product. To say the company is successful is an understatement. Basecamp is profitable, and indeed it has been every year since 2004. It has just over fifty employees, and they are scattered across the world. Jason works out of Chicago, and David lives in the south of Spain. Engagement is high across all team members.

But what makes Basecamp such a unique story is not the collaborative project management product it sells (although it's quite good), but rather the manner in which the company operates. Basecamp employees are time aficionados, masters of staying present, mindful and attentive. They are time behavior experts. It might even be more worthy a cause than the product they hawk

43

that helps millions. It starts at the top with Fried and Heinemeier Hansson—quintessential leaders of self and others.

Fried literally gives a damn about time. He's big on "a good day's work and a good night's sleep."[7] Fried and Heinemeier Hansson insist on running the company as calmly as can be. They don't want stressed-out employees who pull all-nighters. They believe in a maximum forty-hour work week, except for the summer months, when it is reduced to thirty-two. A common mantra at Basecamp is that if a problem can't be solved by five p.m. on a Friday, it will still be there on Monday at nine a.m.

The co-founders instituted "Library Rules," where Thursdays are considered no-talk days. It's whisper-quiet, online and in person. Just like a library. And if that weren't enough, the employees' calendars are private. (You can't book a meeting with a tool like Microsoft Outlook or Google Calendar because you have no idea if the other party is available or not.) Like university professors, Basecamp team members post "office hours" during which they're officially available for meetings and discussions.

It all sounds a bit nuts. But it's only nuts if you continue to think that sleeping with the time enemy is a good idea. Quick reminder: it's not. Also, did I mention Basecamp has been profitable since it launched?

In their most recent book, *It Doesn't Have to Be Crazy at Work*, the co-founders wrote: "A great work ethic isn't about working whenever you're called upon. It's about doing what you say you're going to do, putting in a fair day's work, respecting the work, respecting the customer, respecting coworkers, not wasting time, not creating unnecessary work for other people, and not being a bottleneck."[8]

They don't manage time; rather, they encourage better time behavior. As the CEO and CTO respectively, Fried and Heinemeier Hansson not only set a tone of balance, they don't freak out when things go sideways. Calm is the ruling behavior, not chaos, busyness or tension. There is no "cray cray busy" at Basecamp. They believe that a healthy lifestyle includes getting plenty of rest, taking your vacation time, and enjoying hobbies. It makes for a better life itself. (And this spills over into work.) The co-founders insist on leading this type of life; otherwise, they do not consider themselves leaders: "Workaholism is a contagious disease. You can't stop the spread if you're the one bringing it into the office," they state. "The best companies aren't families. They're supporters of families. Allies of families. They're there to provide healthy, fulfilling work environments so that when workers shut their laptops at a reasonable hour, they're the best husbands, wives, parents, siblings, and children they can be."[9]

Basecamp isn't alone. Take for instance Shopify CEO Tobias Lütke, who wrote: "I'm home at 5:30 pm every evening. I don't travel on the weekend. My job is incredible, but it's also just a job. Family and personal health rank higher in my priority list. We don't burn out people. We give people space. And that's why people show up to work as their authentic selves."[10]

When you misuse your time—and fool yourself into thinking time management is actually a thing—you wind up committing a crime and murdering any chance for mindfulness. But when you realize that navigating your use of time occurs with better behavior—by being present, mindful and focused—you just may end up as calm and engaged as everyone at Basecamp (or Shopify).

The Problem

Time cannot be 100 percent managed, but you can change your behavior to use your time more effectively. (I might state that a thousand times in this lesson.) This is the ultimate problem you must solve. Compounding the challenge, however, is the tendency of leaders to abuse the terms "capacity," "efficiency" and "productivity." When we abuse these words, we abuse our team. We limit our ability to be present, mindful and focused. It erodes relatability. (See Lesson 1.)

Sadly, these terms are an organization's ticking time bomb. Every day, misguided leaders are throwing gasoline on the time fire by applying anachronistic views of capacity, efficiency and productivity. Consider the following comparisons:

▶ **CAPACITY**

What misguided leaders think it means:
The amount of time left to load more tasks onto my plate and my team's plate. "Do more with more."

What it actually means:
The total amount of time people (and I) have available to perform tasks. "Do the same with the same."

Improper Use Example:
After my weekly one-on-one meetings, project meetings, staff meetings, client meetings, status updates and presentations, I have sixteen hours of capacity to do other work. What more can I pile onto the team?

Proper Use Example:

I have forty hours to accomplish my tasks and responsibilities this week. The team has a total of 360 hours to perform tasks this week. How do we make this ethically successful?

▶ **EFFICIENCY**

What misguided leaders think it means:

How I can cut headcount or hours to achieve the same result. "Do more with less."

What it actually means:

How I can improve operational processes or team habits and behaviors to achieve our goal. "Do the same with less."

Improper Use Example:

We will produce five more widgets 20 percent quicker and cut our team by a third while increasing customer satisfaction scores.

Proper Use Example:

We will eliminate any time blockages or clock-wasters that impede our ability to produce the intended number of widgets.

▶ **PRODUCTIVITY**

What misguided leaders think it means:

How I can draw blood from a stone by increasing output through pressure tactics. "Do more with fear."

What it actually means:

How I can alter behavior through engagement measures to increase specific yield factors. "Do more with heart."

Improper Use Example:
We will coerce employees into staying late to meet deadlines. We will not take no for an answer. Otherwise, we will fire them.

Proper Use Example:
We will provide mindfulness techniques to help team members stay focused, engaged and positive in meeting our goals on time.

TERM	MYTH	TRUTH
Capacity	Do more with more.	Do the same with the same.
Efficiency	Do more with less.	Do the same with less.
Productivity	Do more with fear.	Do more with heart.

Let's recap. First, you fail to remember that capacity is actually a math equation. There are only so many hours in a week, but your inability to forecast a) what's on your plate and b) how long it might take to add other items, causes you to constantly work over capacity. (And also the team you might be leading.) It's an emergency call to avoid the stress house.

Second, senior leaders have a tendency to look for "efficiencies" first rather than behavior improvements. In many large organizations, the Cost Efficiency Program (or CEP for short) is used as a smokescreen to eliminate headcount for purported "efficiencies." Often it's a sham. I should know; I was privy to it for years. Doing the same with fewer people or cutting an employee's hours leads to stress, disengagement and customer satisfaction issues.

CEP only saves money; it doesn't improve efficiency or employee engagement.

Third, when you use fear as the tool of choice to improve productivity, you're as foolish as those who thought Cheetos Lip Balm was a good idea. Productivity improves—and profits correspondingly increase—when you lead by caring. (See *Ideas for Making Change Possible* below.)

5 LEADERSHIP QUESTIONS TO ASK YOURSELF

1. Do I understand the importance of controlling my time rather than having events control me?
2. Do I understand the importance of blocking off time to think, prepare and get caught up?
3. Do I understand the importance of sleep, wellness and mindfulness techniques?
4. Do I know the difference between capacity, efficiency and productivity, and how they are interrelated?
5. Am I a workaholic?

Why Staying Present Matters

It's no wonder the biggest driver of workplace stress is workload.[11] Leaders and employees alike cannot seem to change their behavior when it comes to the concept of time. A nerve-wracking workload is the result. Even the World Health Organization has taken notice.[12] It considers "burnout" an occupational hazard "resulting from chronic workplace stress that has not been successfully managed." It characterizes burnout across three dimensions:

· Feelings of energy depletion or exhaustion;
· Increased mental distance from one's job, or feelings of
  negativism or cynicism related to one's job; and
· Reduced professional efficacy.

If the World Health Organization is concerned about people burning out at work, you know it's become a serious matter. Signs that you are a burnout statistic should be self-evident, but just in case, a few insights are given below.

The costs of workload and the related poor behaviors around time are adding up. Researchers estimate that in the US alone, $48 billion in additional annual expenditures are attributed to workload-related stress issues.[13] Research conducted in the United Kingdom found that 15.4 million days per year are lost due to work-related stress.[14] Workload is the number one reason. The cost to employers is in the hundreds of millions. Gallup's research with workers showed that those suffering from workplace burnout are "63 percent more likely to take a sick day and 2.6 times more likely to be actively seeking a new job."[15]

Marianna Virtanen of the Finnish Institute of Occupational Health discovered that employees who work in excess of eight hours per day are 12 percent more likely to become heavy drinkers. Furthermore, she found that increased workload is a direct risk factor "for the development of shortened sleeping hours and difficulty falling asleep."[16]

You need sleep. It's really important. Reading those bogus articles highlighting leaders who get by on four hours of sleep is comical. Those people are an anomaly. Stop comparing yourself to them and please don't look up to them as heroes. For example, research conducted by the US military suggests "losing one hour of sleep per night for a week will cause a level of cognitive degradation equivalent to a .10 blood alcohol level."[17]

Indeed, we are "cray cray busy," and it's now affecting both our health *and* the bottom line. In summary, the increase in workload is causing you to drink more, sleep less, add pounds to your figure and escalate your stress level, all the while causing an impact on the organization's bottom line and customer satisfaction.

Seriously, why the hell do some people still believe in the "do more with less" myth?

YOUR "STAYING PRESENT" QUOTIENT MAY BE IN PERIL WHEN:

You think that work-life balance is a myth.

You believe that things are happening so fast these days, there's just no time to plan.

Mindfulness techniques are for those who read the Chicken Soup for the Soul books. You don't need eight hours of sleep a night either.

You believe people have infinite capacity. If they don't demonstrate it, you don't need to work with them. (You may even fire them.)

There is only one work ethic, and that is being "on" all the time. There is no need for an off switch.

Go to www.LeadCareWin.com/scorecard *and assess your Stay Present score. It will only take a couple of minutes. Then return to the book.*

Ideas for Staying Present

In 1926, Henry Ford, founder of Ford Motor Company, discovered that if he decreased daily working hours from ten to eight in his factories—and shortened the workweek from six days to five—the output of his employees increased.[18] As zany as it must have seemed, after a successful trial, Ford implemented the change across all assembly lines. Pundits and competitors were shocked. Naturally, most businesses soon adopted it.

In the end, both Ford—as the leader—and Ford Motor Company employees benefitted significantly. To be clear, it wasn't a time management practice; it was a behavior change. It wasn't until 1936, some ten years later, that the New Zealand government formally reduced ordinary working hours per week from forty-eight to forty.

New Zealand? Why bring up New Zealand? It's simple. There is a fantastic example we can learn from when it comes to changing the time-related behavior of an entire organization versus tugging on capacity, efficiency and productivity levers. And it originates in New Zealand.

Perpetual Guardian is a knight-in-shining-armor example of good time usage. The company of roughly 250 people is a provider of estate planning services across New Zealand. They've been in business since 1882 in one way, shape or form. The firm offers planning options to thousands of New Zealanders, be it wills, trusts or other advisory services. In fact, it administers assets valued at over $150 billion.[19]

In early 2018 it began thinking about time. Specifically the company wondered if it was squandering its employees' use of time during the workweek. It questioned if the forty-hour work-week was too much. (Take that, Henry Ford!)

Senior leaders at the firm started considering chopping off a day of work from the workweek. They began a trial program where every employee was to work a four-day week. Same amount of work, performed in four days. The results were as you might guess. How'd they do it? It's a lesson in changing behavior as it relates to time rather than simply trying to be better at time management. Behavior change tends to win long-term over capacity, efficiency and productivity levers.

In one of the trial cases, employee engagement rose by 40 percent. Corporate and individual client feedback remained the same or improved even when employees worked eight less hours a week.[20] Employees further recommended that meetings be cut from sixty to thirty minutes. In addition, agendas are now a part of every meeting to keep people on track.

The original forty-hour workweek at Perpetual Guardian was not squished into four days such that people began to work ten-hour days. Everyone from the CEO down has found a way to change their time behavior. Tasks and job functions that used to take forty hours are now accomplished in thirty-two, spread over four days.

Employees became more present, mindful and focused. They were more attentive to one another. One of the biggest impacts was how team members created more collaborative and social relations amongst themselves. Many indicated that they wanted to help each other out more and share their work in the four-day model. Confidence shot through the roof. The company wrote:

"Initiatives like the Four-Day Week give workers the gift of time and the gift of being able to look after themselves and reconnect with families, and we know policies like this are starting to make a difference in people's lives."[21]

Shifting to a four-day workweek may sound extreme, but it's the overarching example of behavior you can learn from. Perpetual Guardian didn't aim to do more with more, more with less or more with fear. It didn't aim to increase capacity, efficiency or productivity. It aimed to change its behaviors so time was better spent. In return, employee engagement went up, customer satisfaction is the same or better, collaboration increased and general mood at the firm shot higher. What's not to like about a behavior change?

Similar to Basecamp, Perpetual Guardian chose quality of life (and work) over a punishing, demanding, nonsensical way of using time. They chose to focus on the *behaviors* related to time.

Consider the following time behavior suggestions for *yourself* first:

Me Time: Analyze your calendar and determine where you can block off time to dedicate to undisturbed, focused work. Perhaps there is a thirty-minute segment at the beginning and end of each working day that is yours, used simply to catch up and plan. Maybe you're able to institute the same for Friday afternoons. Whatever you decide, "Me Time" is a time behavior that protects you from feeling overwhelmed by having too many meetings and too much busy work.

Be Fully Present: During one-on-one or group meetings, be fully present to others. This means 100 percent attention. Don't check your phone or answer that text, or pretend you care while concurrently editing a presentation file on your laptop. Don't put your phone on mute while on a conference call only to lose track of what the conversation is about. ("Sorry, I was on mute," is the oldest trick in the not-paying-attention-to-the-conference-call book.) Give your undivided attention so nothing is lost. In doing so you won't be forced to catch up after the fact, seeking to sort out what you missed (which ends up wasting more time in the end).

Mindful: In the age of being always on and constantly busy, you might introduce "mindfulness practices" to your day. Consider, for example, a ten- to fifteen-minute segment during lunch where you grab some earbuds, put on some instrumental music, close your eyes and simply take some deep breaths in a vacant room. Or take a short walk outside the building or around your neighborhood by yourself, clearing your mind from any work-related actions. Mindfulness practices can aid your ability to be focused and present when it's necessary to be around other people.

Email/Texting/Phones: Consider what your personal response time should be when it comes to these forms of communication. Maybe you choose to only respond at certain parts of the day versus instantaneously. Maybe you have certain rules set up for your boss or key team members on a mission-critical project. Create a personal communication habit and stick to it. (And let your colleagues know what they can expect of your communication norms.)

Sleep: Stop pretending you can get by on four or five hours of sleep a night. It's unsustainable and bad for your health. According to the National Sleep Foundation, healthy adults require between seven and nine hours of sleep per night.[22] (In turn, this will help you tackle time behaviors at work.)

NOMOFOMO: FOMO is the "fear of missing out"; however, when applied to time behavior, it's your opportunity to simply say "NOMOFOMO!" (No more FOMO.) You don't need to be involved. It can range from excusing yourself from recurring meetings, to dropping yourself from project status updates, to office socials that might impact your ability to complete a task. Saying NOMOFOMO— and eliminating FOMO—is a behavior modification that eliminates infringements on your time that might be considered superfluous.

Summaries: Alfred Sloan, CEO of General Motors from the 1920s to the 1950s, established a time behavior known as the follow-up memo. After a discussion with people, the memo contained the high-level points, conclusions, decisions and any assigned actions that transpired. It was itemized for Sloan's record-keeping as well as any other employees involved. It becomes a time behavior life saver, ensuring you don't run around after a meeting trying to figure out what was decided. (And yes, you can use any number of useful apps for the summary.)

When leading *others*, contemplate the following recommendations:

Time Audit: Assess how employees are spending their time. What are the total number of hours in meetings, communication (emailing, texting, calls, etc.) and status report updates versus the employee's actual role-related tasks? Getting a handle on the total amount of time spent by team members gives you a better sense of what's really happening time-wise.

Meeting Audit: Assess all types of meetings to determine how many are happening per month, how many people are in them and what their duration is. Furthermore, evaluate the meetings themselves and decide if there are meeting conduct improvements to make (e.g., agendas, notes, summary actions, etc.).

Communication Audit: Assess how people are communicating with one another. Building on the *time audit*, evaluate where there are over-communication and under-communication habits that add to workload and workplace stress. Texting, for example. How often are employees texting, for what work-related purpose, and what are the response-time expectations around your texting culture? I find too many organizations do not define it, so everyone thinks they must immediately answer texts.

Project Audit: Analyze how long projects are truly taking to complete. Assess a sample size of projects to determine what operational processes are working and which ones are broken.

Stress Audit: Ask employees how they are feeling. Without a good sense of their mental and physical wellness, you won't have an understanding of any workload-related stress or pressure issues.

Capacity Audit: Assess how much work is actually taking place. Projects, production, trialing, servicing, researching, etc. How much actual work is occurring versus the total number of hours available to the team or organization?

Bureaucracy Bomb: By virtue of the various audits that you have performed, work with the team to drop a bomb on any bureaucratic (a.k.a.: behavioral) items that get in the way of the team's performance, operating practices and use of time. Be ruthless—cut any nightmarish and time-wasting behaviors out.

Team Norms: It is imperative that you and the team establish behavioral norms when it comes to working together. I call them *team norms*. Basecamp provides a few examples, such as Library Rules Thursdays and Office Hours. They may not be for you, but the creation of norms is key. Clearly articulate what you and your team expect of each other in terms of how you approach time. Hold one another accountable. If you do nothing else as a leader of others when it comes to time, establishing team norms is the best behavior change to try.

Four-Day Workweek: It's potentially a stretch goal, but if Perpetual Guardian and Basecamp (in the summer months) are able to do it, maybe it's something for you and your organization to consider.

"The present moment
contains past and future.
The secret of transformation,
is in the way we handle this
very moment."

Nhat Hanh
Understanding Our Mind,
Parallax Press, 2006

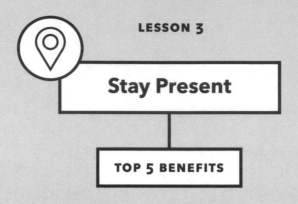

LESSON 3

Stay Present

TOP 5 BENEFITS

1. Applying new behaviors (rather than managing time) puts you in charge of your time.

2. Your capacity is better understood; staying constant versus becoming overloaded.

3. Stress levels can be reduced while energy levels could potentially increase.

4. Family and personal time will improve.

5. Your overall morale and engagement at work will be better.

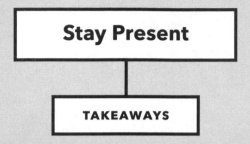

Stay Present

TAKEAWAYS

Me Time: Analyze your calendar and determine where you can block off time to dedicate to undisturbed, focused work. Be consistent.

Team Norms: Clearly articulate what is expected of everyone on your team in terms of how you approach time and its related behaviors. Be collaborative.

Email/Texting/Messaging/Phones: Decide what your personal response time should be when it comes to email, texting, messaging and phone calls. Be unfailing.

 Visit www.LeadCareWin.com/extras *for recommended books, essays, videos, quotes, songs, poems and art related to Lesson 3: Stay Present.*

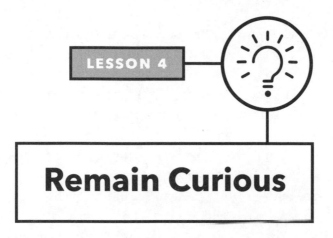

LESSON 4

Remain Curious

WHEN I WAS an adolescent, I used to read the dictionary. Weird, I know. I wouldn't tell anyone for fear of being mercilessly ridiculed. I told my teenage children that story one day, and they laughed their heads off. Something was clear to me, though, in my formative years. I understood early on that improving my vocabulary was the key to "getting ahead," or whatever I would have called it back then. So I read about words (and truth be told, I still do).

I also read poetry and song lyrics. The experience often felt the same. Delving into Rudyard Kipling or mid-eighties Canadian music acts like Corey Hart and Rush escorted me into an infinite reservoir of words and related emotions.

During my elementary school days, I'd purposely find different classmates to walk home with, even taking longer routes as a result. I was deeply fascinated by their stories and dispositions. Some were troublemakers, others were unpopular. A few were challenged in one form or another.

One boy in particular, Tim, had a severe learning handicap coupled with a speech impediment. No one wanted to walk with Tim. However, when we ended up strolling to his house, he was not shy about talking about his day, his brother, his mother and home life, which proved to be troubled. He would tell the most amazing stories, some of them made up and typically having to do with *Star Wars*. He'd chat to me with a perpetually runny nose, often wiping away the nasal discharge with his bare arm. However, I chose not to see through Tim; I chose to see him through, all the while enhancing my understanding of people.

Another boy, Ian, was occasionally mocked by others in grades seven and eight. He possessed a lisp and a rather uncoordinated body. Whenever I walked home with Ian, I'd end up learning about his passion for technology and inventing things. He was as curious as Benjamin Franklin. He often got me thinking. Ian also unknowingly moved me to action.

As an eleven-year-old, I begged my father for a computer. The year was 1982. In part because of Ian's curiosity and penchant for inventiveness, I reckoned I should learn how to use a computer. If Ian was technologically savvy and curious, I should be too. At the time of my dad's eventual purchase of a TI 99/4A computer—the most magnificent piece of equipment to hit my home at the time—the only programming I could do to make it work was in the language of BASIC—Beginner's All-purpose Symbolic Instruction Code. I'd spend hours typing in thousands of characters to make a stick man jump across the screen. Eventually I'd buy a copy of *PC Magazine* and follow pages and pages of line-by-line BASIC code to build a mock US election strategy game. Despite Reagan's historic victory at the time, the Democrats seemed to win more frequently in my game.

A few years later, a soccer injury forced me to undergo knee surgery. I spent nine months rehabilitating the knee with various physiotherapists three to four times a week. Those too were productive conversations about health, the body and the medical field. It drove me to acquire a copy of *Gray's Anatomy*, the bible on all things medically related. I was sixteen. That book changed the way I thought about the interconnectedness of our bodies. I didn't read it all—it was far too complicated—but again, it got me thinking. It got me learning. It got me thinking about becoming a doctor.

When I attended McGill University to attain my undergraduate degree in education—after forgoing studies in the medical field—naturally there was a fair amount of formal learning. After all, it was a degree program. There were loads of professors and classes. However, I craved more. I felt the urge to complement the institutional components with other means, experiential in nature. I'd often venture out on the metro in Montreal, pick a place in the city I'd never visited and discover it. The vast richness of a neighborhood and its inhabitants became an eye-opening and visceral learning experience. My broken French came in handy when necessary.

Throughout my working days in the public sector and corporate world, I've challenged my thinking and knowledge level in many different ways as well. Some of those methods will be explored later in this chapter as recommended practices. The purpose of taking you through part of my personal life here is to say that from a very young age I've never been afraid to explore and learn outside of a classroom. I have always been inquisitive. My curiosity remains unabated to this day.

I consider myself a "lifelong learner" not because I possess a bunch of degrees, certifications and formal coursework, but because I have remained interrogative, acknowledged my weaknesses and filled any gaps by using counterintuitive methods. My intent has never been to turn myself into the smartest person in the room. If I am, I'm in the wrong room.

It's all about your attitude. At the risk of excessive modesty, I believe my lifelong learning approach is one of my greatest strengths as a leader of self and others. It has a lot to do with how curious I am. Harvard Business School professor Francesca Gino discovered, however, that only 24 percent of leaders across the globe feel curious in their jobs on a regular basis.[1] That means three-quarters of us aren't inquisitive, a statistic that astounds me given a leader's need for clarity of foresight. (See Lesson 7: Command Clarity.)

Having access to other people's knowledge is like walking through an ancient forest of intelligence. Maybe you hook up with a mentor or coach who helps you see things differently. Perhaps you're part of a book club or regular social gathering where you interact and learn from one another. The people you surround yourself with—and those you invite to become a part of your inner learning circle—are as critically important to your acumen as any other modality.

To become a lifelong learner, you need a mindset shift. It starts with you and your curiosity aptitude. This is the challenge I now put forward to you.

The Problem

Time is one of the enemies of lifelong learning (recall Lesson 3: Stay Present). When you lack the space to ruminate, marinate, dialogue and deliberate, you forgo the opportunity of intellectual and emotional advancement. Furthermore, a lifelong learner is calculated. If you think learning happens by way of a breeze, you have missed the point of being an intentional learner. The increase in knowledge occurs when we are deliberate.

Nelson Mandela was a lifelong learner. Now there's a man who understood the term, who was habitually curious. As a prisoner on Robben Island, he was the consummate example of continuous self-improvement through voracious learning. Not only would he devote himself to a constant flow of new knowledge by dedicating the time, but he would also rally those around him to do the same. He organized what was known as Struggle University at the prison, where he and his fellow inmates created a host of curriculum options for each other, be it mathematics, politics, science or philosophy. Study circles were prevalent. All of it was purposeful.

Mandela always made time for people, too. He never dehumanized, as there was something to learn from everyone. The commitment to making time and being intentional with other human beings was a necessary criterion for him. Before being incarcerated, for example, Mandela spent many hours not only garnering several degrees but ensuring he took the time to listen to people's stories and learn about their backgrounds. Whether with professors, lawyers, tribe leaders, commoners or Afrikaner politicians, he would spend hours learning through dialogue. You might say he was dialectical.

He employed the same tactic in prison. Mandela would often be seen chatting with prison wardens and guards, asking thoughtful questions about their upbringing. He may have been more educated, but he never considered himself the smartest person in the room, even in jail.

Hold on to that thought of Struggle University. In 2012, Pakistan's Malala Yousafzai was shot in the head by the Taliban for clashing with their restrictions on female education. She was fifteen years old. For several years prior, Yousafzai had been fighting for equal rights to education, pleading her case on blogs and in media appearances. Yousafzai provides a poignant example of the critical importance of lifelong learning and curiosity. She was not about to let her life pass without an education, without access to knowledge. She fought to learn. In 2014, she won the Nobel Peace Prize for her efforts. Learning requires fight, a fight to overcome the incessant demands of time-wasters, naysayers and self-doubt.

There is another problem that impacts lifelong learning. It's called "spray and pray."

Intuitively we know that learning is a good thing. In many cases, leaders are throwing loads of cash at the problem. Total investment in organizational learning on a global basis has been on the rise since the early 1980s. In 2020 the industry is estimated to be worth over $250 billion. About 10 percent gets spent on outside products and services (content like LinkedIn Learning and Harvard Business eLearning), another 35 percent accounts for training expenditures such as travel, facilities and equipment, while a final 55 percent is doled out to pay for the people who deliver and develop the training.

The real problem is not the investment, but what happens *after* the learning takes place. As a recovering chief learning officer, I see this all the time. Let's review a real-world example.

One beautiful Tuesday, Sally attended an excellent one-day workshop on customer service. Her boss was a supporter of the idea. She learned all about the importance of reliability, responsiveness and relationships. It was an enjoyable day of learning, full of activities and great dialogue. The facilitator was top notch.

There was a smorgasbord of food for breakfast, healthy snacks at the morning break, sushi for lunch, and another break in the afternoon with Häagen-Dazs ice cream. When the day finished, people stuck around to network, sipping Napa Valley wine.

All told, Sally's session with thirty of her colleagues broke down as follows:

· Six hours of learning, activities, self-reflection, table group exercises and discussion.
· Three hours of networking, food, breaks, drinks, etc.

The hard costs for the one day of training came in as follows:
· Facilitator: $12,000 (including travel costs)
· Food & catering: $3,000
· Venue rental: $2,500 (including Wi-Fi, A/V, etc.)
· Employee travel costs: $10,000 (six employees flew in for the session, the rest drove to the venue)

The opportunity costs for one day of training were as follows:
· Thirty employees
· Assume an average salary of $80,000
· $306 (the cost per day of training based on their $80,000 annual salary) × 30 employees = ~$10,000

The one day of training for thirty people ended up costing the organization roughly $40,000.

The investment itself for the one day is excellent, but the problem rests with what came *after* the wine stopped flowing. The typical next step for most organizations is that nothing else happens. Leaders lose sight of the investment, consider it a "job well done" and don't prioritize anything further. More time or intentionality to ensure the learning has a positive impact on the team member gets overlooked. Thus, there is no behavior change. The team member goes back to their job, inundated by regular tasks, overrun by the usual time constraints and lacking any further fight to embed the new learning in their existing work habits.

The $40,000—although somewhat useful—ends up being wasted. It's where the line "spray and pray" comes from. The one day of training was sprayed out with a fire hose by the facilitator to those in attendance. Leaders then prayed that whatever was taught somehow might have magically been absorbed (and applied) by the team members in attendance after the training finishes. By Friday, Sally wasn't using any of the facilitator's nifty customer service suggestions.

Spray and pray: it's mainly getting down on your knees as a leader and desperately wishing that the investment isn't all for naught. It's how lifelong learning gets wasted. We don't take new learnings and apply them to change our workplace habits.

In summary, the problems that can pop up with our learning rituals are as follows. We are:

Too cautious: We can be too timid to try different ways in which to boost our brainpower.

Time stressed: We don't prioritize learning as a key factor of leadership. (Whether our own learning or that of those we are leading.)

Pedestrian: We don't push ourselves to meet other people, pausing to learn from them.

Smug: When in a leadership role, we assume that, due to our fancy title, we know best.

Apathetic: We lack the fight to embed newfound knowledge by changing existing habits (e.g., spray and pray).

Ignorant: We fail to address the development needs of employees we are leading.

Overburdened: We're just too busy to learn.

---

5 LEADERSHIP QUESTIONS TO ASK YOURSELF

1. How often do I reach out to other people for their ideas, stories and knowledge? Ultimately, how curious am I?
2. How often do I make the time to learn? Daily, weekly, monthly, quarterly, annually, never?
3. Once I have learned something, do I commit to embedding it into my leadership style?
4. Am I positively encouraging those I lead to learn, develop and be curious? How?
5. Do I fully understand the benefits that accrue because of lifelong learning?

Why Remaining Curious Matters

When you commit yourself to lifelong learning—with the appropriate change to a perpetually curious mindset—your prospects for improved leadership capabilities open up. Of course, your level of competence increases, and so too does your confidence. People tend to gravitate to those who exhibit quiet self-assurance, not loud arrogance. No one wants to be led by the know-it-all who is also afraid to admit their mistakes, someone so arrogant they claim they don't require any further learning. (Recall Lesson 1: Be Relatable.) Being in a room with a cocky smarty-pants is as welcome as a house flood.

A curious, discreetly confident, question-asking, always-learning attitude is one that people tend to look up to. A learning leader with this attitude inspires others. When you think of Stephen Hawking, other than his sheer brilliance, you have to tip your hat to how curious he was to learn about new concepts. He was deeply admired for his inquiring mind. Marie Curie was not only the first woman to win a Nobel Prize, she was the first person to win a Nobel Prize *twice*. She did so in two different sciences, physics and chemistry. You can't win a Nobel in science (twice!) and lack curiosity. Walt Disney was another example. He once said, "Around here, however, we don't look backwards for very long. We keep moving forward, opening up new doors and doing new things, because we're curious... and curiosity keeps leading us down new paths."[2]

Your commitment to lifelong learning will likely spawn new ideas while increasing creativity levels. I alluded to Benjamin Franklin's unquenchable curiosity earlier in this chapter. His pledge to learn something each day produced some of the world's greatest inventions. Franklin dedicated one hour to his personal learning every weekday. Furthermore, as a twenty-one-year old, he created a discussion group called Junto. Franklin described Junto as a group of "like-minded aspiring artisans and tradesmen who hoped to improve themselves while they improved their community."[3] It was a place of learning, of collaboration, ideation and curiosity.

When you commit to learning continuously—while embedding any newfound skills or traits into your leadership style—it demonstrates your intentionality that the status quo is never good enough.

When I was a chief learning officer developing the TELUS MBA program in conjunction with the University of Victoria—a two-year master's program explicitly dedicated to TELUS, my place of work for ten years—I handpicked the advisory committee. After a few sessions with the group discussing the program framework, one of the committee members took me aside. "Dan, I really like where this program is heading. Do you think I might be able to apply for it?"

The individual was already a vice-president at the company. They possessed twenty years of career and professional success. Frankly, they were already a rock star, but decided to leave the advisory committee and submit an application. The submission was approved. Two years later the VP graduated.

The individual had this to say about the learning experience: "One of the best decisions I have ever made was to apply to the TELUS MBA program. Doing an MBA at this stage in my career helped me to embrace the latest insights and research in our ever-changing, constantly transforming business marketplace." The status quo for this leader just wasn't good enough. And changing that status quo reaped benefits for the hundreds of team members, partners and community stakeholders who were guided by this leader's newfound knowledge and behaviors.

Fast-forward a few months. I was thinking about one of the team members I was directly supporting. In particular, I thought the TELUS MBA might be an excellent developmental complement to their existing skillset. It turns out that the idea of an MBA hadn't even crossed their mind, let alone the TELUS MBA. "I think you should apply," I encouragingly said one day. "You'll learn a ton, make some new contacts, and you'll be able to apply your learnings to your current role, and whatever might come next."

That team member was accepted into the program. Even before graduating, they were offered a new role within the international arm of the organization. It was a straightforward decision. As this team member's leader, I was proud to recommend the program and prouder still to see the team member's achievements with a whole host of differentiated responsibilities, projects and opportunities. The bird had flown the coop, so to speak.

Taking care of your lifelong learning curiosity habit is vitally essential, but as a leader of others I find it equally imperative to look out for those you lead, even if it means they might leave for a new career nest.

YOUR "REMAIN CURIOUS" QUOTIENT MAY BE IN PERIL WHEN:

You don't think of your team as a source of ideas. You believe that ideas worth investing in come from the top of the organization.

You learn only as much as you need to in order to do your job. You're not interested in learning much else.

You believe too many new ideas are just too risky and out of your comfort zone. You don't want to try anything new that has the chance of failing.

When people need your help, you're not that curious about what they're up to.

Work is work and not school. There's no sense of throwing away money on learning that is frivolous.

Go to www.LeadCareWin.com/scorecard *and assess your Curiosity score. It will only take a couple of minutes. Then return to the book.*

Ideas for Remaining Curious

Judith McKenna, president and CEO of Walmart International, once said, "Businesses have to commit to lifelong learning, not only in hard skills but also in soft skills."[4] McKenna is right. But how? I propose five tactics:

▶ LEAD OFF

▶ ENGAGE

▶ ADAPT

▶ REINFORCE

▶ NURTURE FORWARD

▶ **LEAD OFF**

Learning needs to become a habit. It needs to be timetabled. It needs space. Your curiosity mindset as a leader should include being able to *lead off* with learning. A baseball team has a lead-off hitter, a batter that is expected to lead off the first inning by getting on base. It's a team norm, hence the title "lead-off hitter." If you're not assuming the habit of leading off with learning—adopting regimented conduct— you're missing out on the opportunity of professional growth.

When leading people, your willingness to help their overall development is another example of how you should lead off. Ask them about their interests, goals and ambitions. Discuss where their performance gaps or deficiencies lie. These are aspects at the very heart of your curiosity. Make certain it's an ongoing, consistent conversation. Be their coach. Encourage them to lead off with learning, too. Help your team members recognize the critical importance of a lifelong learning mindset.

▶ **ENGAGE**

Franklin's example of Junto is a powerful one. So too is Mandela's desire to meet people from all walks of life, learning from their stories and backgrounds. When you *engage* with other team members or contacts—even pushing yourself to meet new colleagues, departments, partners, customers, suppliers or competitors—potential knowledge is at your disposal. Make it a habit not just to network but to meet with people who possess expertise in areas where you are weak. To engage with others is to tap into a friendly curriculum that is boundless. Set up coffee chats, webcam sharing meetings or discussion forums. Make it a regular part of your calendar.

Similarly, those you lead will need the occasional push to engage with people outside your team. As a leader, you have the opportunity to set up some of those encounters through your network. For example, if someone on your team is quite nervous about public speaking, find an individual in your circle who can assist. Maybe a team member has planned a vacation to Italy. Why not introduce them to someone you know who is the resident expert in all things Italian? Your leadership does not need to be restricted to the workplace.

▶ **ADAPT**

American Alice Coachman won the Olympic gold medal for high jump at the 1948 London Summer Olympics. She was the first Black woman to win Olympic gold in any sport. The catch? She had to *adapt* to succeed. Due to the racial segregation of the day, Coachman was forbidden to train with white people. Instead, she figured out how to perfect the high jump using materials she could cobble together, like sticks, ropes and crates. She even trained barefoot. Take Coachman's lead and adapt. You cannot rest solely on your laurels or existing intellect. Nor will the road ahead be easy. Always be on the lookout; take stock of what you know and what you need to know (the gap), and be mindful of adapting to achieve it. The modality could be anything, be it a course, coach, TED Talk, book (hint, hint), podcast or game. The depth, breadth and timing of any learning are also factors that can influence how you might adapt.

The same can be said for those you are leading. Your team members require a leader who pushes them in the direction of adaptation. Some of them may get stuck in a rut, too afraid to try new methods by which to learn. Their sense of urgency may not even register on the meter. They may not know that there are other ways in which to augment their knowledge. Whatever the factor, your responsibility as a leader of others is to help them see their blind spots. Get them to adapt their existing habits to become a lifelong learner, hopefully just like you.

▶ **REINFORCE**

As with the example of Sally at the customer service training workshop, if you fail to *reinforce* the new knowledge or insights into your leadership habits, you might as well have poured the investment straight down the gutter. This is the point at which you actualize newfound wisdom. While there is no one-size-fits-all rule, what I recommend is to regularly write down the critical behavioral bits from any new learning that you have consumed, in whatever modality. Review those notes often and then weave the ones that make sense into your leadership practices. I was introduced to the Evernote application in late 2008. Shortly after that, I changed the way I stored ideas in my head as well as ideas found on the web, in meetings, classrooms, on my bike, wherever. Since then, other people have taught me different and better Evernote techniques. Had I ignored the first opportunity to weave Evernote into my leadership habit or failed to be open to new ways in which to use the application, I might not be as organized as I am today.

▶ NURTURE FORWARD

Pay homage to the maxim "pay it forward." When you *nurture forward*, you do two things. First, you are continually seeking to nurture yourself by being curious to learn about entirely new concepts. As with Hawking, Curie and Disney, inquisitiveness ought to be one of your leadership differentiators. When you nurture forward, you aim to step out of your comfort zone to build up competence in areas where you are weak or need assistance or that you should be curious about. Basketball player Shaquille O'Neal is a sublime example. Not only does he possess a BA, MBA and Ph.D., but Shaq also studied cinematography simply because he didn't know anything about it. He trained to be a mixed martial arts specialist because he thought it might help him, not in basketball but in life. Police officer? Sure, why not? He cultivated that skill, too, by becoming a volunteer officer. He also took up acting lessons and studied the innards of financial investing. O'Neal has always been curious, a lifelong learner nurturing forward his blind spots.

This now brings us to the second facet. For a leader of others, to nurture forward is to make sure you are tending to the development path of your team members. I'm against the annual performance review meeting, which generally comes with the yearly career development chat, too. That's as useful as a VHS rewinder. It's soul-destroying, too. Your conversations with team members must be timely and frequent. If you're truly nurturing forward, you're also sending along relevant articles, podcasts, videos, books (hint, hint again) and even thoughts on formal courses. Maybe those suggestions resolve a current gap. Perhaps they—like Shaq's pursuits—relate to areas that might not otherwise be contemplated by the team member. In either case, your role as a leader is to nurture forward as consistently and as helpfully as you can.

If you were being super curious, you already know that the five lifelong learning tactics make up an acronym that spells LEARN. If you didn't notice it, don't worry. I had no clue what "tl;dr" meant until the day I asked one of my teenager's friends. (It means "too long; didn't read," by the way. Hopefully that does not apply to you and this lesson.)

"Learning proceeds until
death and only then does
it stop.... To pursue it is
to be human, to give it up
to be a beast."

■ **Xun Zi**

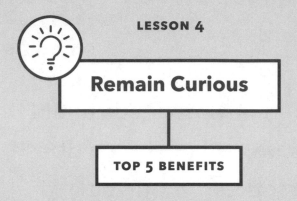

Remain Curious

TOP 5 BENEFITS

1. You wind up smarter, more engaged, and able to truly call yourself a "lifelong learner."

2. Curiosity becomes a consistent personal habit, and an admired leadership trait.

3. No longer are you the smartest person in the room; you are an unpretentious yet inquiring apprentice.

4. Your desire to meet people—getting to know their backgrounds and knowledge—increases your credibility.

5. The investment you make—be it time, money or relationships—is not wasted; it compounds.

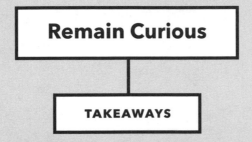

Remain Curious

TAKEAWAYS

Adopt a lifelong learning mindset.

Begin using the LEARN tactics.

Be curious in all that you do.

Visit www.LeadCareWin.com/extras *for recommended books, essays, videos, quotes, songs, poems and art related to Lesson 4: Remain Curious.*

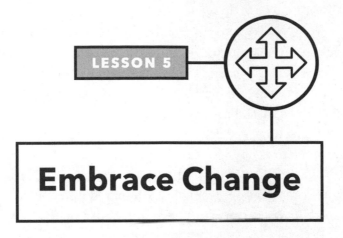

Embrace Change

I'VE BEEN WRITING this book for over a year now. I'm privileged to live in Victoria, on Vancouver Island, where a good deal of my composing and contemplation takes place. Due to Victoria's latitude, I get to experience four seasons every 365 days. It's now fall again, and the leaves are slowly beginning to change color. What a wondrous palette of reddened hues currently staring back at me. I hope to wrap up the book by the end of next winter, which means I will have experienced six seasons over eighteen months of authoring. As I stare out the window, pondering the seasons, two words come to mind, ever so critical to leadership: *embrace change.*

The phrase is easy to say—embrace change—but much harder to employ.

Take for example the story of Kodak. In April of 1880, George Eastman founded what would become Kodak, a firm made famous for its camera products and photographic film. I distinctly recall the company's advertising push, during my youth, to make everything a "Kodak moment."

Everything *was* a Kodak moment in the 1980s. Casual conversations turned into Kodak moments. It was Instagram before Instagram. Kodak encouraged us to celebrate the moments of our lives. All of them. Specifically, they wanted you to do it through the magic of Kodak film.

For a long time, Kodak was by far the ubiquitous and dominant brand of photography.

Over the course of nearly 150 years, the company has seen its fair share of change, roughly six hundred different seasons. Although Kodak is still in business—and traded on the New York Stock Exchange (NYSE)—it's somewhat shocking to take note of what the company once was, what was at its fingertips, and what it sadly became.

Kodak entered bankruptcy protection in 2012. Two years prior, it was delisted from the S&P 500 Index. At its height, Kodak employed 120,000 people. Today, there are only five thousand employees. Kodak suffered losses in the hundreds of millions of dollars. It used to be the number one camera and film company in the world. In the US alone it sold upwards of 90 percent of all photographic film as well as 85 percent of all cameras to consumers and businesses. It dominated in all sectors of its space. Bankruptcy protection? It's not possible. It's unthinkable.

Experts tell us that a failure in leadership is often the root cause of a company's demise. Did Kodak's leadership fail the company? Did leadership fail in not adapting to change over the course of a century and a half? One might say, "Of course Kodak embraced change; it's been around for 150 years, averted bankruptcy, and is still traded on the NYSE." Yes, you might say this. But what if you knew that Kodak was responsible for inventing the first-ever handheld digital camera? The original prototype weighed eight pounds and took twenty-three seconds to record the image to tape. But it was theirs. A key trait of leadership is having vision, a grip on the future. It appears that Kodak checked that box. And then the company ignored it altogether and failed to change.

The year was 1975, and a twenty-four-year old Kodak engineer by the name of Steve Sasson was spending time in the lab, sorting out how to create a digital photo. In the end, he designed the world's first digitalization process, with electronic pulses from a lens converted to binary code, which then was stored to tape—the images displayed on a television screen for all to see, at least all those in the lab.

No paper, no film, no messy, dingy darkrooms to produce Sasson's photographs. It was the world's first digital camera and digital photography. Displayed directly to a monitor, it was a modern-day technological marvel. There was no film! Sasson received a patent for his work in 1978.

He started to demonstrate the new invention to groups of Kodak executives across all business units. Sasson saw the future and wanted to share the good news. His enthusiasm was palpable. There was one problem, however. The sound of crickets was considerably louder than his senior leaders' and executives' excitement.

Why were leaders so averse to Sasson's invention? Even though they allowed him to continue working on newer and more technologically advanced prototypes, he was forbidden to speak publicly about his work. They licensed the technology and made some money off of the patent, but executives refused to alter Kodak's overall course. They felt Kodak was a print photography business, nothing else.

The problem comes down to change—specifically, an aversion to it.

Instead of embracing Sasson's creation and becoming first-to-market with digital cameras, executives insisted that their bread-and-butter products—still cameras and film—would remain the business model. It was a colossal mistake, an egregious failure to see how the company's technology could impact and improve the consumer's experience. Ease of use and instant gratification? What was there not to like? The leadership's near-sightedness and refusal to change caused the company to nosedive. Kodak has been trying to recover ever since.

In an ironic twist, the first digital camera that Sasson made is now on display at the Smithsonian National Museum of American History. Also, in 2009, Sasson was awarded the National Medal of Technology and Innovation. Oh, what Kodak could have been if leaders hadn't fought change. Instead, Sony and Canon went on to dominate the market until smartphones made the mass market digital camera (mostly) obsolete.

Of course, there is a similar story that could be written about Research In Motion (now BlackBerry) and its comparable unwillingness to embrace change. As with Kodak, BlackBerry dominated the mobile smartphone market. Reluctant to see that business users would ever want a digital camera embedded in their phone, the company watched their massive market share disappear in a matter of quarters. Apple and Samsung shot past it with superior, user-friendly devices with built-in cameras. If I were cheeky, I might say it was a "Kodak moment" for leaders at BlackBerry.

Staring out the window for the past eighteen months, I've watched the seasons change. Throughout the passing of six seasons, I've had to embrace the dampness, wetness, cold, wind, fog, humidity and sunshine. Sure, it's only weather, but it's a metaphor.

As a leader of self and others, no matter the situation, you have to embrace change, or that book might never get written. That goal you're trying to attain may never get achieved. That team you're leading may never improve its results. Much hinges on how you embrace change.

I insist that you not make it a Kodak moment.

The Problem

If the Kodak story wasn't enough to convince you about the importance of embracing change, perhaps some insights into our natural aversion to change might. In my career experience working with thousands of leaders and employees as well as through the research I've come into contact with, I have found there are six roadblocks to successfully embrace change.

▶ ROADBLOCK 1: Being a Negative Nancy

It's not your fault; you're just hardwired to be negative. (And you don't have to be called Nancy.) People have an automatic bias and a higher sensitivity to adverse thoughts. In the case of Kodak executives, their belief that no good would come of the digital camera invention—and that it would negatively impact sales of still cameras and film—was the company's undoing. Kodak execs wore their pessimism proudly. In the end, their fear of losing outweighed the opportunity to change and even have bigger wins. "Better the devil you know than the devil you don't know."

▶ **ROADBLOCK 2: Stupid Is as Stupid Does**

Made famous by the film *Forrest Gump,* "stupid is as stupid does" is a line that haunts many of us. The bottom line is you don't want to look stupid in front of your colleagues, or worse, your superiors. It's completely understandable. To take a chance on doing something different or recommending a new idea means putting yourself out there. You're risking your reputation. A mental math equation ensues: "Should I risk everything for fear of ridicule and the chance I might fall flat on my face, or should I just keep my head down?" If you do choose to keep your head down, it's showing the white flag, a failure to embrace change. "Stupid is as stupid does" is not the reputation you want, so you abstain from contemplating any type of change.

▶ **ROADBLOCK 3: Engaging in Camp Groupthink**

Groupthink is defined by social psychologist Irving L. Janis as "A mode of thinking that people engage in when they are deeply involved in a cohesive in-group, when the members' strivings for unanimity override their motivation to realistically appraise alternative courses of action."[1] Its definition is backed by historical references like the Bay of Pigs invasion, the failed Pearl Harbor defence, the Swissair collapse, and the Watergate cover-up. In short, groupthink is a change for the sake of change actioned by blind, group-based consensus. It's embracing the wrong type of change, and for the wrong reasons. When you make a judgment far too quickly without adequately assessing all aspects of the decision—while your colleagues go along for the same narrow-minded ride—you wind up with a poor decision and a drastically detrimental end result.

▶ ROADBLOCK 4: What's Old Is Comfortable

Do you have a favorite pair of jeans you refuse to throw out? Does your desk contain items that might be from a decade ago? Do you have an app that you refuse to delete on your phone? Are you a creature of tried-and-true habits? When we get accustomed to a way of doing something, changing the pattern requires more energy because alternatives can be ambiguous. It requires more energy, more brainpower. If you commute to work in a car, how often do you choose a different direction? When you go for lunch, do you try a new restaurant or a new item on the menu? You might be sticking to what's comfortable. There's nothing wrong with that, per se, but when it comes to future-proofing your leadership skills, remaining in those old jeans and using the same, potentially antiquated habits is not indicative of a leader who fully embraces change.

▶ ROADBLOCK 5: Being a Lazy Pants

Change can be a time-gobbler, a voracious one. When there is a choice between engaging in change versus maintaining the status quo, you'd be surprised how often the latter wins. A CEO I was working with once announced a new direction for the company that encompassed an organizational restructuring. After they made the announcement, the project never got off the ground. One executive—who was roughly twenty-four months away from retirement—complained incessantly of the work required to change how their business unit would have to operate if the org restructuring took place. Another executive looked at the task at hand and decided to take early retirement. Your degree of laziness and mental apathy can easily get in the way of embracing change.

▶ **ROADBLOCK 6: Quitting Because It Failed Once Before**

J.K. Rowling submitted the manuscript for *Harry Potter and the Philosopher's Stone* to twelve different publishers before it was accepted. What if she had quit sending her book after receiving five rejections? Ten? Steven Spielberg was denied entry to the University of Southern California School of Cinematic Arts three times. What if, as a result, he decided moviemaking was not his thing? When an idea has previously failed, I find that some people, unlike Rowling and Spielberg, tend to let sleeping dogs lie. There's no point in pushing the idea forward, because it's bound to fail again. When we observe others fail, it only compounds our thinking. If it failed once, it will fail again, or so many of us think who are not named Rowling or Spielberg.

---

5 LEADERSHIP QUESTIONS TO ASK YOURSELF

1. Do I ever reflect on how well I cope with change?
2. Am I fully aware of the change that is occurring in my organization or industry?
3. Do I ever think that change might be hard on my team (or others) and that they might need my support?
4. Do I agree that embracing change is simply the right thing to do?
5. Do I blame others for not adapting to change, when in fact there are other factors at play?

Why Embracing Change Matters

Your capacity for growth and role success is commensurate with your willingness to embrace change, because within change there is opportunity. There are many reasons people dislike change, some of which are listed below and may account for the bog you are mired in. I have been mired more than once in my life.

After two years of teaching high school, I decided to leave the profession to learn more about the blossoming high-tech world of the late 1990s. That then landed me a leadership role at an institute of higher education. I soon went back to school again, this time earning an MBA, which led to a leadership role with a high-tech company. After six years, I pivoted once more, venturing into the telecommunications space as a chief learning officer. Five years later, I brought to market a customer-facing, culture-change consulting firm—from within the same telecommunications company. After another five years passed, I decided to embrace change once again and launched my own leadership development strategy firm, the Pontefract Group. Throughout the latter three roles, I wrote four books.

Each of these career decisions of mine required the inclination to embrace change, to enter the unknown. That willingness has not only deepened my level of competence (and confidence), but it has developed an army of colleagues and contacts I can call on at a moment's notice for assistance. My network has become my net worth as a result of my ability to embrace change (see Lesson 6: Dare to Share).

But I'm certainly not perfect. There are plenty of examples where I didn't fully embrace change, squandering an opportunity for growth. It tended to result in stress, pain and unnecessary anger.

For example, our family moved from Vancouver to Victoria in 2011. My lovely wife, Denise, had accepted a director's post at a school there. The two cities are separated by one hundred kilometers and a large body of water, and I was somewhat miserable for the first three years. Vancouver lies on the mainland. Victoria sits on an island. We depend on a ferry, helicopter, floatplane or airplane to get on and off the island. There is no bridge. As of this writing, the *Star Trek* transporter remains a dream as well.

I travel a fair bit for business. When travel happened, I wanted the trek home to Victoria to be shorter. I desperately desired the commute time to be the same as it was to travel to and from Vancouver. Quite simply, I didn't want to embrace the change of actually having moved cities, and the fact that my travel pattern had to alter, too. I possessed a fixed mindset. It caused a fair amount of needless grief between me, Denise and our three children. Had I embraced the change better and sooner, I might have enjoyed more of my first three years living in Victoria. I may have met more people to add to my network earlier. Thankfully, I smartened up, embraced the change, turned things around in 2014 and haven't looked back since.

During the financial meltdown of 2008 and 2009, I was asked to trim $6 million from a corporate budget. That's a lot of money. The initial shock took its toll on me. In hindsight, instead of being dazed and confused for several days, I should have fully embraced the request and quickly moved into collaboration mode with my peers and teammates to address the edict. In essence, I was numbed by spilt milk; there was nothing I could do to alter anything. The milk was spilt. The CEO had made a decision. My job was to get on with things. I learned from that moment that decisions made at the top of the organization are ones you really can't alter. You may not agree with them, but it's not your place to disagree. Embracing change is key to accomplishing your task with grace, quality and speed. It preserves your sanity, too.

YOUR "EMBRACING CHANGE" QUOTIENT MAY BE IN PERIL WHEN:

You believe you do not have the time to embrace change because you are too busy doing your "real job."

You think your industry could never change to the point where everyone's job would be in jeopardy.

You only embrace change if it's a policy or legal thing.

Your rule about making change happen is to wait for it to happen and then address it.

You tell yourself you know what needs to get done and by when. It's other people who don't get on the bus. Change fails to happen because of them, not you.

Go to www.LeadCareWin.com/scorecard *and assess your Embrace Change score. It will only take a couple of minutes. Then return to the book.*

Ideas for Making Change Possible

Sir Winston Churchill was a savvy and intelligent leader, at least in my books. Words he spoke in 1924 during an exchange in the British House of Commons continue to resonate with me long after I discovered them: "There is nothing wrong in change, if it is in the right direction. To improve is to change, so to be perfect is to have changed often."[2]

Before outlining a few helpful techniques, let us first agree that change is inevitable. Think of change like the English language. Was the word "chatbot" around in 1955? No, it arrived in the mid-1990s. Now it's commonplace. It's a change.

What about "bird"? Today those winged creatures we see flying around are known as birds, but in Old English they were referred to as "brids." Over time, the pronunciation morphed to "bird." It's another change. No one puts up a fight with words like "chatbot" and "bird" nowadays. They naturally evolved into our everyday vernacular.

If as a leader, you accept that change is inevitable, you will have won half the battle. Nothing ever stays the same. When you remain entrenched in your views, unwilling to recognize the good that can come as a result of doing something different, you're as likely to accept "chatbot" in your dialect as you are to wonder why the classic Beatles song wasn't titled "Blackbrid."

▶ **PLUCK FROM YESTERDAY, FOR TOMORROW NEVER KNOWS**
In another homage to the Beatles, to embrace change you should frequently review what has worked or not worked in the past, aiming to take those lessons forward. You pluck the learnings of

yesterday, because tomorrow never knows when those learnings will influence a new project or decision. If you think of completing a project as an example of change, write down three things that went well through the project and three that did not go so well. Keep the notes handy. Before starting another project, review the notes. Furthermore, if a change arrives on your doorstep, not of your doing, don't immediately react. Go back and revisit your "lessons learned" notes and see if any of them will help you adjust to changes in pattern or behavior that will unavoidably arrive.

▶ THERE WILL BE BUMPS IN THE ROAD, SO LISTEN UP

The American Psychological Association (APA) discovered that only 43 percent of employees have confidence that any workplace change has the desired effect initially intended by senior leaders. People have a general reluctance to a) accept change, and b) believe that change will produce a positive or beneficial result.[3] You have a responsibility to a) accept not everyone is on board to a change right away, and b) understand there is no such thing as frictionless change.

Like you, people have different tolerances for change, opinions on its merits, and questions of intent. To smooth out the inevitable bumps in the road, take the time to listen. Listen to the rationale of those who might have initiated the change. Try to make sense of it, and then move on. If you are leading people, listen to the fears or angst that they may possess. Lend an empathetic ear. (Recall Lesson 1: Be Relatable.) Employees often require the chance to emote or vent their frustration before being receptive to any type of change. Provide a listening conduit for that to happen.

▶ REFRAME YOUR THINKING

BlackRock is a global investment management corporation. It's the world's largest, managing assets of roughly $7 trillion as of 2019. Founded in 1988, the firm was deeply committed to the profits of the companies it served. After all, that's how it makes money. Black-Rock believed fully in the theory of maximizing shareholder return.

But a change in thinking began to take shape in 2011, when BlackRock shifted its investment practice from one "predominantly focused on proxy voting towards an approach based on engagement with companies."[4] By 2018, BlackRock's CEO, Larry Fink, went further, suggesting the company would only invest in firms that believed in creating long-term value. In 2019, Fink doubled down and said BlackRock would look to align with companies that demonstrated a sense of purpose, because "society is increasingly looking to companies, both public and private, to address pressing social and economic issues."[5] In 2020, Fink went one step further and indicated BlackRock would put "sustainability at the center of our investment approach."[6] BlackRock wasn't always a leading pioneer in the reshaping of business, but now it is. And that came as a direct result of not only embracing change, but having the willingness to reframe how things have always been done. It's a stark lesson: Are you set in your ways and thinking, or are you open to different approaches?

▶ THE BRIGHT SIDE OF SPILT MILK

When working with executives, I often emphasize the need for humor while keeping things positive during periods of change. During the change, it is inevitable that milk will be spilled. Instead of complaining or immediately taking a contrary position, my advice is to do everything in your power to look at the bright side.

My wife and I have a few "family proverbs" that we've used for years. One of those, "Everything always works out," is a bright-side framework. When a move to a new city isn't quite working out as planned—as when we moved from Vancouver to Ottawa, only to endure a treacherous ice storm, among other issues—we chose to look at the bright side of the experience. "We've never experienced an ice storm before," we'd say. "What's it like to live in minus-20-degree-Celsius weather without any heat in your home?" Similarly, prior to 2020 and the outbreak of the coronavirus SARS-CoV-2, we had not experienced a pandemic of such impact. Quarantined for weeks on end during the spring months with three teenagers, we took the opportunity as a family to write songs, start a board game tournament, bake a new dessert nightly and plant a vegetable garden for the first time ever. Your ability to embrace change also partially rests on your keenness to see the bright side of any unwelcome scenario. How you coach your team members on this subtle yet vitally important aspect will help them adjust to the change as well.

▶ **SOS—ASK FOR HELP**

When the RMS *Titanic* rubbed its belly against an iceberg, personnel in the communications room were immediately asked by Captain Edward John Smith to send Morse code distress signals. When *Apollo 13* ran into difficulties on their mission to the moon, Captain James Lovell famously communicated, "Houston, we have a problem." When Ada Lovelace ran into mental blocks with her computer programming, she didn't hesitate to reach out to Cambridge mathematics professor Charles Babbage for assistance. As we have discussed, things will inescapably go sideways. My advice is to treat these deviations to your plan as merely another opportunity to embrace change. Instead of trying to sort out the issue on your own, however, swallow your pride, embrace the unintended change and request assistance. Who are the go-to people within your domain who might help you with the unanticipated issue that popped up? Who can help you get things back on track? It's also another example illustrating the importance of maintaining a robust yet diverse network of contacts. Ask for help.

"Change always involves a
dark night when everything
falls apart. Yet if this period
of dissolution is used to create
new meaning, then chaos
ends and new order emerges."

Margaret Wheatley
"Leadership Lessons for the Real World "
Leader to Leader Magazine, Summer 2006

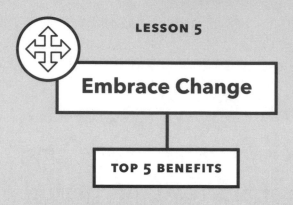

LESSON 5

Embrace Change

TOP 5 BENEFITS

1. Life becomes less stressful, and anxiety reduction is likely to lead to productivity increases.

2. When unanticipated curveballs head your way, you shrewdly know how to address them.

3. Others around you recognize your capacity to adapt, admiring your flexibility and poise.

4. You will experience growth, able to use it in future scenarios when change is thrust upon you.

5. You're no longer pusillanimous of change, but rather a leader who embraces it as seamlessly as the seasons change.

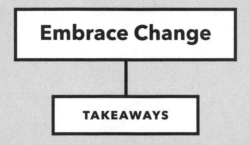

Embrace Change

TAKEAWAYS

Accept that change is a constant; there are four seasons for a reason.

Stay positive, open, flexible and patient when change inexorably arrives at your doorstep.

Embrace change and use it as a potent leadership skill in your dealings with others.

Visit www.LeadCareWin.com/extras *for recommended books, essays, videos, quotes, songs, poems and art related to Lesson 5: Embrace Change.*

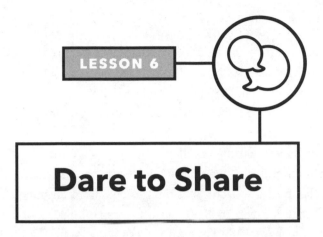

Dare to Share

SITUATED IN the Gulf of Mexico, about forty miles off the Louisiana coast, the *Deepwater Horizon* drilling rig was a marvel of technology and safety. Built by South Korean company Hyundai Heavy Industries, the rig—owned by Transocean—was a renowned deep-water semi-submersible mobile offshore drilling unit. I know, it's a mouthful. The simple version is that it sucked oil in abundance from below the deep ocean waters.

The folks on the rig knew their lives depended on attention to safety. As of April 2010, multinational oil and gas company British Petroleum (BP) was proud to report that the rig had zero "lost-time incidents" during its seven years of operation under contract to BP. "Lost-time incidents" is a standard Occupational Safety and Health Act (OSHA) metric that calculates the number of events that result in time away from work. In essence, there were no safety issues whatsoever. Moreover, the oil kept coming.

On April 20, 2010, the unthinkable happened. Not only did the rig's safety record evaporate by virtue of a disastrous explosion, eleven of the 126 onsite crew members lost their lives. Furthermore, by the time the damaged wellhead (known as Macondo) was capped, an estimated 4.9 million barrels of oil had spilled into the Gulf of Mexico. That's over 210 million gallons. The rig eventually sank to the bottom of the sea. As you can imagine, the environmental repercussions were staggering. It remains the most massive accidental marine oil spill in history. It was a catastrophic loss.

Several inquiries were launched to probe the accident. Arguably, the most important was the National Commission on the BP Deepwater Horizon Oil Spill and Offshore Drilling. Established by President Obama about a month after the incident, the bipartisan commission was tasked with "providing recommendations on how the United States can prevent and mitigate the impact of any future spills that result from offshore drilling."[1] The chief counsel's report on the disaster provides insights into the significance of how (and when) we share information with colleagues. The report is also an indictment on the negative repercussions of hoarding knowledge and failing to impart or transfer experience.

Myriad issues led to the *Deepwater Horizon* accident. Several were technical in nature. The most damning, however, came down to people. Specifically, leaders. The summary report stated, "While many technical failures contributed to the blowout, the Chief Counsel's team traced each of them back to an overarching failure of management."

The investigation proved that, with three different sets of employees from three separate companies (BP, Transocean and Halliburton) supposedly working together on the rig, a lack of collaborative leadership was at the center of the accident. "All three companies failed to communicate key information to people who could have made a difference," wrote investigators.

As I dug further into the commission's findings—and the multitude of other reports and data points made available to the public—it became evident to me that those management failures bore common threads. To my consternation, an obvious bias existed amongst employees to *not* communicate with others. They operated in silos, despite their claim to put safety first.

Worse, there was blatant hoarding of intelligence, knowledge and prior learnings. When crucial information and experience are kept from others, negative consequences are likely to ensue. *Deepwater Horizon*, albeit profoundly tragic, is a masterclass leadership case study in a catastrophic failure of sharing.

Those BP employees who worked in offices were aware of the risks the drilling site posed from a safety perspective. They did not convey those risks to the rig workers, or to colleagues at Transocean or Halliburton. Appalling? For certain, not to mention unconscionable.

BP and Transocean were brought on the carpet for failing to communicate lessons learned from previous drill site experiences. Investigators concluded that prior learnings of employees who worked on different rigs and sites could have assisted onsite decision-makers on the *Deepwater Horizon* rig, perhaps mitigating the risk of an explosion. Those who withheld said knowledge have to live the rest of their lives knowing eleven people were killed due to an unfathomable preference to hold back vital intelligence.

There were numerous other examples of poor judgment in sharing. Employees purposely determined *not* to proactively seek out information before making a decision critical to everyone's safety. It's like reverse hoarding. It's also an example of ignoring the potential benefits of new information. When you assume you have all the knowledge to make a decision, you have decided to go with your own bias and reject information that would change assumption into an evidence-based decision. You have decided to dismiss your colleagues by not sharing information.

In the case of *Deepwater Horizon*, investigators found that "decision-makers often failed to seek counsel from others with expertise and instead made decisions based on incomplete information." Again, a silo mentality.

When we hoard or ignore information and knowledge, the results can often be scandalous. In this example, on the Gulf of Mexico, it was deadly. *Deepwater Horizon* helps us understand the critical importance of sharing as a key leadership lesson. The commission's summary findings underline the point: "Better management of personnel, risk, and communications by BP and its contractors would almost certainly have prevented the blowout. The Macondo disaster was not inevitable."

The Problem

Deepwater Horizon is a terrible tragedy. It's a genuinely horrible story. However, I needed to get your attention when it comes to the problems associated with not sharing. When you operate in a vacuum or a silo, there can be an almost infinite number of issues that crop up. It ultimately negatively affects your ability to lead self and others appropriately. Unsurprisingly, it is the opposite of caring.

Not only might there be a deadly calamity—as was the case with *Deepwater Horizon*—you might be putting yourself, colleagues or your organization at risk of completing objectives. When information is knowingly withheld, it can become tremendously difficult to move forward with a task. It's at this point that the pressure begins to mount personally.

Picture yourself at work. You've been waiting for a file from a colleague for two days now. The original request was sent via a friendly email. That file contains vital client data that was to be used to support a follow-up discussion with a customer. The meeting is now tomorrow. Instead of three days to prepare, you now have less than one—and you still don't have the file!

Instead of being adequately prepared, you are left scrambling. That data was crucial to the discussion. You followed up several times with your colleague, only to be ignored or stonewalled. As the clock ticks, you feel your level of stress rising. The cortisol begins to seep into your interactions with other people at work. You're not yourself. You have become a ball of tension. Rather than enjoying a family dinner the night before the presentation, you're left working late into the night to finalize it. You're burning the midnight oil, all because a colleague decided to operate in a silo.

Now flip things around. What if that colleague were you? What if you were the one who was lazy and chose to ignore the email? What if you elected to harbor ill will towards your colleague for some alleged oversight from a year ago that you heard through the grapevine? There was no proof, just water-cooler talk. You believed it and in return acted childishly. What if you dismissed your colleague's request, thinking it was unimportant? What if you not only overlooked the request but ignored the fact that you had even more information that would have given your colleague some timely assistance?

A personal challenge that's critical to solve is the entrenched biases we bring to work. These often lead us to operate in a silo, unconsciously (or consciously) withholding know-how vital to the other party's success. These biases often get in the way of sharing. We buy into myths. We neglect to dig deeper into the half-truths. We believe that Charlie in accounting did, in fact, steal Jamie's lunch from the fridge, so we're not ever going to answer his direct messages. (It wasn't true. It was the boss, Sarah, who ate the lunch.)

Sometimes entire departments are given a label. The marketing department is full of weirdos. The IT team is unfriendly, always saying no to my request for a new laptop. The sales team is slipshod, constantly over-promising and under-delivering. The finance group is so dull, never having any fun. The researchers are nerds and don't talk to anybody. I can't even speak the same language as the engineers. Why does tech support keep me on hold for twenty-three minutes?

Whether there are individual, team or departmental biases, they can become a massive problem in our efforts to share information, data and knowledge with others. Moreover, this is one of the biggest problems to solve as a leader of self and others.

Due to some pretty deep-seated biases among different parties attached to *Deepwater Horizon*, the three companies were guilty of concealing data and knowledge from one another. BP even withheld information from its own people. In the end, it resulted in a deadly environmental catastrophe.

Individual biases in the workplace are very effective at creating a moat around us. "Why on earth would I want to help them?" we might say. Only certain people are allowed to cross the bridge. Others are left outside the castle's walls. We don't even throw them a personal flotation device. It's a massive problem in the workplace, one that offers a significant opportunity in your quest to become a leader who cares.

5 LEADERSHIP QUESTIONS TO ASK YOURSELF

1. Do I understand that problems are solved in what lies between me and my colleagues?
2. Do I understand that innovation, growth and action happen quicker when organizational knowledge is distributed?
3. Do I understand that information needs to be freely shared for actions to be swiftly completed?
4. Do I understand how important feedback is to getting things done?
5. Do I understand that my stakeholders (peers, customers, partners, citizens, etc.) expect timely and correct results?

Why Sharing Matters

There's a line about drinking alone and feeling lonely in Billy Joel's classic song "Piano Man" that gives us pause to consider the significance of sharing.

When we work alone it can indeed become an isolating, empty feeling. During the pandemic, millions of workers were forced to work from home for the first time. Levels of employee loneliness became deafening across the globe. It's why the act of sharing is one of the advantages to a more caring form of leadership. It's a bit like the Horace Mann quote: "A house without books is like a room without windows."[2]

A house (or room) needs windows to allow the sunlight in. Otherwise, aside from manufactured light, we live in darkness. But so too, the windows allow those who live in the house to look out, to observe the world and its external splendor. The window serves as a two-way contract. Sharing matters because leadership is about continuously operating through a window. There is an expected partnership, an exchange.

When you fail to share your knowledge or information with others, you not only inhibit your ability to lead, but you also impact the professional development of your colleagues. Also, when you do not ask for someone else's data or expertise, similarly you wind up alone, isolated with ignorant thinking. You're on a dead-end street. You end up trying to look out a one-way mirrored window. It's a bit like those ones found in police interrogation rooms you see in shows like *Homeland*.

Sharing is at the very heart of leading self and others. If you remain unwilling to share, something nasty could happen, and you just might find yourself at the center of it. It may even become a broken window.

YOUR "SHARING" QUOTIENT MAY BE IN PERIL WHEN:

You hoard information, especially new information, because that's how you think you can get ahead.

You are unconcerned about the potential impact of failing to share information with your organization.

You believe that voluntarily sharing information with others is only for those who work in Human Resources.

You never need to ask for help. Asking for help is a sign of weakness.

You blame your organization for hiding information from you. So, in return, you withhold information from your colleagues.

Go to www.LeadCareWin.com/scorecard *and assess your Sharing score. It will only take a couple of minutes. Then return to the book.*

Ideas for Becoming Better at Sharing

The call center I was observing was a hive of activity. Men and women were busily chatting, supporting one customer inquiry after another. A headset adorned each agent's head. In front of each agent were two computer screens. One contained the customer's details, while the other showcased an array of simulated displays to help the agent work through the problem.

Each interaction was jovial. There were loads of light-hearted exchanges. Between the friendly banter and queries, something else was happening. The agents I observed were multitasking on their mobile phones. It took me a while to figure out what they were doing. They weren't updating Facebook or Instagram. No, instead they were texting. Why on earth would they be texting in the middle of a support call? That's just as bad, isn't it?

"They don't let us use instant messaging," said the team member. "They think we're goofing off. We can't even access the wiki. We have to use that during our breaks or training days."

The "they" this employee was referring to were their leaders. In management's infinite wisdom, they thought it would be a good idea to prevent the call center agents from accessing the company's instant messaging system, even though sharing knowledge is at the root of leadership itself. Instead, the team members employed a work-hack. They worked around management's incompetence and ignorance.

The employees knew that if a support system were set up so that they could share information and help one another answer questions, they would be more productive and a lot less stressed. So that's exactly what they did. Management didn't even realize it was happening. It turns out that the organization's so-called leaders didn't understand the importance of sharing or understand how a collaborative workplace could benefit their business. They just didn't care.

To change how you share, consider changing how you view sharing itself. I recommend three types of sharing: up, down and around.

▶ **UP:**

You have information, data, experience and knowledge that are vital to *other* people's success.

STOP:

· Keeping files locked away on your computer.
· Deleting texts, emails and voicemails that might help someone else.
· Assuming people don't want (or need) your expertise and knowledge.
· Believing your stuff is too good to be shared with others.
· Being apathetic, looking the other way when others are in need.

START:

· Uploading your non-confidential files to a shared folder or cloud drive for others to access.
· Reflecting on how random acts of giving may positively impact others.
· Imparting your knowledge by coaching or mentoring others—whatever allows people on the team to learn from your past experience.
· Asking others what they might need from you to be successful. (Be a giver!)
· Thinking about the needs of others when it comes to the information you hold. (Remember, empathy is one of your greatest assets. See Lesson 1: Be Relatable.)

▶ DOWN:

You have information, data, experience and knowledge that are missing yet equally important to *your* personal success.

STOP:

- Believing you are the smartest person in the room.
- Assuming other people are too busy to help you out.
- Pretending colleagues don't have data or expertise that can assist.
- Worrying about hierarchies and job titles; information is information (hat tip to *wirearchy*).
- Acting like you operate on an island; you are not a misfit or outcast.

START:

- Recognizing that sharing is more significant than the sum of its parts.
- Creating a habit of asking people for help, insights or their data regularly. (Be ego-less: see Lesson 2! And don't be afraid.)
- Politely asking others to submit their files and documents to shared folders or cloud drives. If you use platforms like Microsoft 365 or Slack or Basecamp, ask people to share pertinent folders.
- Taking the initiative to get people to teach you things that you don't know about or understand (go for a lunch-hour walk or coffee, or have a short coaching session).
- Branching out and building a stronger or more extensive network; the better your network, the easier it is to access data and knowledge that you don't have.

▶ **AROUND:**

You have information, data, experience and knowledge that are critical to the *organization's* success.

STOP:

· Participating in the water-cooler myths that feed mistrust across teams and prevent sharing.

· Believing that the non-sharing actions of one are representative of everyone.

· Thinking your information is more substantial than another department's.

· Using "I'm so busy" as the excuse for not sharing your data or knowledge.

· Assuming someone else is probably sharing the information. (What if they're not?)

START:

· Willingly blogging or commenting on internal platforms about what you know. (Others may not have heard of you, but your knowledge may well be useful.)

· Ending meetings with a simple question: "Can I provide you with any other data points or information that might help?"

· Forwarding emails or texts to people that can help to connect dots.

· Donating time to your organization's learning and development team: be a trainer for a subject-matter area that the organization could benefit from.

· Introducing people in your network to other employees in the organization. (Contemplate using the adage "my network is my net worth.")

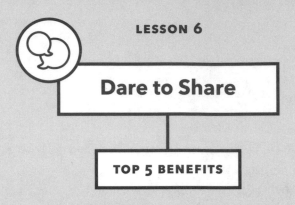

Dare to Share

TOP 5 BENEFITS

1. If you are a giver of information and wisdom, your colleagues become smarter and are far more likely to address their specific objectives, tasks and goals.

2. The organization operates with dexterity and agility, possessing the ability to deal with potential issues promptly. (Not to mention innovating and spawning new ideas at a faster rate.)

3. You feel good. Giving away information and knowledge to help others will release the hormones dopamine and oxytocin. (They're the kind of hormones that make you feel good.)

4. Becoming unafraid to ask others for information demonstrates your vulnerability, something we don't see enough of in today's leaders.

5. Sharing is caring. (I know, it's a tad cliché and right out of kindergarten, but it really does make sense.)

Dare to Share

TAKEAWAYS

Drop the pretense: find ways to publish or make publicly accessible your non-confidential files, data, etc. for team members to benefit from.

Offer up your experience to colleagues in the organization. Be a mentor, or at least someone who shares their knowledge.

Begin asking your peers for any information or wisdom that might help your objectives. Don't be shy.

Visit www.LeadCareWin.com/extras *for recommended books, essays, videos, quotes, songs, poems and art related to Lesson 6: Dare to Share.*

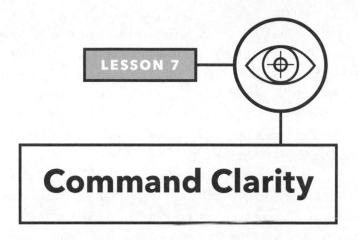

LESSON 7

Command Clarity

"**EUTHYMIA.**" **IT'S A** magical word, one we've purloined from the Greeks and altered for twenty-first-century purposes. The word was first used by the philosopher Democritus to describe an important aspect of life: cheerfulness. We should operate with a little more joy in life, or so thought Democritus. U2's Bono once claimed that Charles Manson stole "Helter Skelter" from the Beatles. Half a breath later, he said that the band was "stealing it back." Maybe it's time to steal euthymia back, too. As I edit this book at the beginning of the coronavirus pandemic, I *really* think it's time to steal it back.

These days, euthymia is more commonly linked to healthcare. Technically, of course, the word wasn't *stolen*, but it certainly morphed away from Democritus' meaning. Specifically, euthymia is defined as "a stable mental state or mood in those affected with bipolar disorder that is neither manic nor depressive."[1] Suffice to say it's not the definition that I want you to remember. (And nothing against those who suffer from bipolar disorder. After all, I witnessed one of my aunts ail from it.)

Enter another philosopher, Seneca the Younger, one of Rome's leading intellectual figures in the mid-first century. He built on Democritus's interpretation of "euthymia" and tweaked it ever so poignantly. In Seneca's essays on tranquility, he defined it as: "Believing in yourself and trusting you are on the right path, and not being in doubt by following the myriad footpaths of those wandering in every direction."[2]

Maybe what Seneca saw in Democritus's definition is that trusting you are on the right path nurtures mental clarity, not having to suffer from anxiety-producing doubt. In the context of strategy and getting things done, this means being mentally alert to goals, having trust and confidence in the team, and being resolved to maintain the set direction in a disciplined way.

This means that there is legitimacy and transparency to your everyday demeanor. The team needs to see and know it is the "real" you, that credible leader who keeps distractions at arm's length and is able to maintain a laser focus. You stay the course, steering the ship forward through choppy waters, ignoring those who encourage you to sail abroad. You command clarity. But don't forget joy. Indeed, there's the need for a little cheerfulness, too.

"Euthymia" is now *your* word. You are stealing it back.

So what happens when we do take our eye off the map, off the ship's wheel? Are there personal, professional or even organizational consequences when we fail to use strategic, decisive and clearly focused dexterities in our actions?

Look no further than lists like the S&P 500 or Fortune 500 as evidence. For example, more than one-third of companies listed on the Fortune 500 in 1970 had been acquired, merged, dissolved or broken into pieces by 1983. Corporate longevity for companies listed on the S&P 500 has dramatically fallen. In 1964, they had been in business for thirty-three years on average. By 2016, that average lifespan had dropped to twenty-four years, and will dive to twelve years by 2027.[3] Household names like Yahoo!, DuPont, Bed Bath & Beyond, Alcoa and Staples are but a smattering of companies that have dropped off the S&P 500. The so-called "retail apocalypse" is rife with examples of leaders veering off the clarity cliff.

Small business is faring no better. Although these companies are not publicly traded and can't be found on any 500-type lists, according to JPMorgan Chase & Co., 51 percent of small businesses in the US are ten years old or less, and 32 percent of them are five years old or less.[4] The bad news is that approximately a third of all new businesses fold within their first two years, and half close up shop within their first five years. In Canada, research conducted by Business Development Canada suggests 51 percent of all new small businesses do not make it past their fifth year either. An astonishing 98.2 percent of all companies in Canada employ fewer than one hundred employees.[5] Thus, small businesses are the workforce engine of employment for the majority of Canadians, yet half of them can't make it past five years.

The public sector is interesting to analyze, too. In Portugal, researchers found that cost deviation relative to whatever was budgeted for public infrastructure projects amounted to an average of 24 percent.[6] That's right, budget $1 million for a new road or building, and inevitably spend $240,000 more. There are hundreds of public-sector examples where large projects wind up exceeding the budget.

In another study, the reason for such cost overruns within public-sector projects boils down to three factors: technical challenges, over-optimism and strategic misrepresentations. Notice anything? The researchers write: "One might expect that budgeting and scheduling would improve over time as those who manage megaprojects gain more experience, but this is not the case."[7] Be it large, small or public-sector organizations, leaders are taking their eye off the ball, acting with a lack of focus, decisiveness and realism.

Then there is Sweden's Greta Thunberg. She is the epitome of determination wrapped in a sublime layer of genuineness. She's having a little fun along the way, too.

At the age of fifteen, in the summer of 2018, Thunberg camped out in front of the Parliament House in central Stockholm, holding a sign: "Skolstrejk för klimatet." It translates into English as "School strike for climate." She refused to go to school, choosing instead to spend her time protesting her government's carbon emissions output. She did so for three weeks. Alone. No one bothered to join the young teen. "I am doing this because you adults are shitting on my future," she said.[8]

Thunberg's inspiring dedication to fighting climate change sparked a movement. Word began to spread. First, it landed in Sweden, where young people took up her cause. Climate strikes began to happen every Friday. Thousands of young Swedes were ditching school to protest. Thunberg's doggedness eventually broadened her reach to the rest of Europe, and soon after that, the world. It seemed as though she had inspired youth right around the globe with her straight talk and deliberate, vigorous leadership.

Thunberg pulled no punches, no matter the venue. By 2019 the movement was now in full swing. At the World Economic Forum in Davos, Switzerland, that year, she said, "I want you to act as if the house is on fire, because it is."[9] A year later, Thunberg returned to Davos. With her eyes set on the media, she remarked, "I don't think I have seen one media outlet or person in power communicating this [climate change] or what it means. I know you don't want to report on this."[10] At the United Nations Climate Change Conference, Thunberg remarked, "Since our leaders are behaving like children, we will have to take the responsibility they should have taken long ago."[11] In front of the US Congress, she pleaded, "You must unite behind the science. You must take action. You must do the impossible. Because giving up can never ever be an option."[12]

The question comes down to *why*. How can a young teenager's example of strategic decisiveness and clarity inspire millions, yet public-sector projects consistently go over budget? Why are large, publicly traded companies failing to survive, while remaining so disengaged? And how is it that half of all small businesses go belly up after only five years of existence?

At least in part, I argue the answer is nested as one of our nine lessons in *Lead. Care. Win.* Your responsibility is to become a leader who is a visionary. Turning smart ideas into action requires a sound strategy and transparent, data-rich decision-making coupled with resolute authenticity. It comes down to your clarity. You must command it. Bringing joy to your work helps as well.

Greta Thunberg may have Asperger syndrome, but she is downright possessed by euthymia. Clarity oozes from her every action. Believe in yourself, trust you're on the right path and be relentless in the pursuit of your goals. Don't fall into the sway of those wandering footpaths and tangential whispers. Remain focused, be clear, yet do so cheerfully. It's time that you acted a little more like Greta—commanding clarity—while stealing back the word "euthymia" along the way.

The Problem

When you operate from a position of instability—flip-flopping too often with your decision-making, coming across as wishy-washy in your actions, lacking strategic vision—you are acting contrarily to the state of euthymia. You run the risk of either losing credibility or not building credibility. No one will look up to you, let alone want to work with you. It will very likely impact your career mobility, too.

That's the good news. Why? If you continue to act in such a manner, as in the examples previously outlined, you are liable to screw things up organizationally, too. Projects manifestly late. Confidence shattered. Job prospects? Slim. Character called into question.

I am reminded of an exchange with a fellow team member who spoke of how he had been overlooked for promotion several times. Here was an individual who interacted with delight and genuineness when dealing with others. Those interactions were pleasant and cordial, supplemented with copious helpings of kindness. In essence, this individual was a model manager, engaged as can be, treating others with great respect and compassion. Other team members liked him as a person, but his superiors appeared to have their doubts. He was doing everything right, or so he thought.

Three times he had been overlooked for a director role. The concern boiled down to a somewhat weak strategic mindset and an inability to consistently meet clear objectives. "How would you describe yourself," I asked him one day. "Do you over-promise and under-deliver, or are you more likely to be considered an under-promise/over-deliver type of leader?" A blank stare ensued.

I continued with another question. "Do you see the glass as half-full or half-empty, or do you question why the glass was too large to begin with in the first place?" More blank stares.

"When you and your team are tasked with a project," I tried again, "does the team tackle the task efficiently, collaborate well, act with clarity and find ways to not only meet the deadline but perhaps to complete the project ahead of schedule?" Looking for a definitive response, I asked one more question: "Do you and the team enjoy yourselves without getting distracted while working on the project?"

Shockingly, he said he had never been asked questions like this before. My conversation then shifted to explicitly asking about his level of focus and ability to complete objectives while operating with a clear view to the future. "You may be pegged," I continued, "as someone who can inspire their team, but who simultaneously fails to act in a way congruent with director expectations. Directors have to look to the future, act with consistent focus, get the task done, deviate if necessary, provide precision-like clarity, all the while motivating their team along the way."

This individual was indeed well-liked and respected by their team. The requirements for a director role, however, required someone who not only could motivate a team but could look into the future to ascertain what strategies and tactics needed to be in place to improve productivity and results. They had to be able to imagine why the glass was designed to be too big in the first place. They had to be unambiguous. Clarity is all.

Equally important in this example, the director role this individual was trying to win required someone who was able to meet objectives without ever needing to offer an excuse as to why a goal was missed. When one "over-promises and under-delivers," they often talk a good game of setting targets or goals, but failure or lateness or incompletions often result. The objectives may be too lofty and then do not get achieved, or too many distractions enter the leader's space, and the expected date of completion fails to materialize.

It may not be the same as falling off the S&P 500 list or closing business after five years or consistently exceeding a public-sector budget by 24 percent, but failing to achieve a promotion can be attributed to that dimension of credibility, where a lack of strategy, decisiveness and/or clarity will impact credibility and reputation. Indeed, it is another important lesson to heed.

5 LEADERSHIP QUESTIONS TO ASK YOURSELF

1. Am I confident with my current state at work? Do I even know where I want to take my future?
2. Am I able to clearly articulate a coherent strategy, communicating why and when goals need to be accomplished?
3. Do I get distracted by the latest fads and shiny new projects while losing focus on what matters most?
4. Do I have any idea how I am spending my time, knowing the difference between thinking and doing?
5. Do I fence-sit on decisions leaving others (and actions) to hang in the balance?

Why Clarity Matters

Clarity and decisiveness are inseparable from strategic ability, and so are the pillars of an organization's longevity, not to mention your own personal leadership success. You can immediately see the consequences of failing to have clarity. Without it, there is no road map to the future.

Mary Barra, CEO and chairman of General Motors, understands this notion well. In early 2016, she wrote: "The auto industry is changing faster today than it has in 100 years. Many facets of the traditional industry are being disrupted, and we at GM believe this creates exciting new opportunities. Rather than fear disruption, we plan to lead it by developing cars that don't crash or pollute, that reduce congestion and that keep us connected to the people, places and activities that are most important in our lives."[13]

She went "all in," you might say, on two key data points. First, as consumer tastes have shifted towards sport utility vehicles and trucks, Barra let the world know that GM's fleet of vehicles would be different. Utility vehicles were morphing into new models. Second, in an attempt to get ahead of the next consumer car revolution, she shifted GM's vision towards electric-powered and autonomous-driven vehicles.

In essence, Barra did not want GM to become a Kodak or Black-Berry. Perhaps she didn't want GM to become the General Motors of yesteryear. After all, it was her company that declared bankruptcy in June of 2009 after years of rudderless, unfocused strategic thinking. Barra was promoted to CEO five years later.

While looking to the future, Barra acted with sheer determination. In 2019 she shuttered five GM plants across North America, placing over fourteen thousand people out of work. No one said leadership was easy. Throughout her tenure—with a perpetual eye to the future—GM became leaner, lighter, sharper and positively more focused. Bloated was no longer cool. Barra cut popular cars like the Volt, Cruze and Impala to ensure GM's strategic plan was successful. She sold money-losing European brands such as Opel and Vauxhall because popularity contests do not secure your survival.

"When you're doing a job, if you're just passing through, you don't invest," said Barra at Duke University.[14] Wise words. Don't just pass through; invest in a willingness to stick to a strategy, acting with decisiveness and clarity along the way.

YOUR "CLARITY" QUOTIENT MAY BE IN PERIL WHEN:

You believe your future success depends on demonstrating how busy you are today.

You lose focus sometimes, but blame it on competing priorities and being given an unclear strategy.

You are easily distracted by whatever looks cool and sexy.

You take on all projects offered to you. You over-promise, but everyone knows you're a team player and "open for business."

You sit on the fence when it's time to make decisions for fear of making a mistake. The team gets frustrated to the point that people want to move.

Go to www.LeadCarewin.com/scorecard *and assess your Clarity score. It will only take a couple of minutes. Then return to the book.*

Ideas for Sharpening Clarity

Years before Ørsted became the world's largest offshore wind company—holding more than one-third of the global market share—the company was known as Danish Oil and Natural Gas. In 2012, S&P unceremoniously downgraded the Denmark-based company's credit rating to negative, due to a host of issues that saw it fall off a financial cliff. Seeing the crisis unfold before its eyes, the company's board of directors brought in Henrik Poulsen, a former executive at Lego, as the new CEO.

Poulsen looked at the situation as an opportunity to reset the firm's strategy. In a matter of months, he transformed the company's focus from oil and gas to wind-based power. Along the way, he became a case study in how to be a strategic and decisive global visionary, leading with clarity.

Numerous books are dedicated to strategic management and decision-making, but I suggest that improving your command clarity level comes down to five key principles:

▶ 1: CURRENT VS. FUTURE STATE ASSESSMENT

▶ 2: TRUTH TEST

▶ 3: FOCUSED FORESIGHT

▶ 4: LOAD MANAGEMENT

▶ 5: DECISIVE DUTY

▶ **PRINCIPLE 1: Current vs. Future State Assessment**

The first principle is to assess where you are currently heading. Be it personally, professionally or organizationally, have you fully bought into and do you remain confident about your future? As hard as it may be to crystal-ball-gaze into the next several years, if you don't spend time contemplating what may occur, you can be guaranteed that the head-in-the-sand strategy will come back to haunt you. Just ask Kodak or any one-hit-wonder band from the 1980s. Hello global pandemic?

After graduating with a bachelor's of education degree from McGill University in 1994, I thought my long-term future would be in the classroom, teaching teenagers. Had I not spent time in the summer of 1996 wondering whether high school teaching was where I wanted to be thirty years later, I most definitely would not be writing this book. Like Poulsen and Ørsted, you have a responsibility to assess whether your future—or that of your team and organization—requires alteration. Your current state may not be a worthy future state. Be ruthless in your assessment.

▶ **PRINCIPLE 2: Truth Test**

How clear are you with both the strategy and how to achieve it? Strategic, decisive leaders are also transparent. They are honest with themselves and those around them. It is worth repeating that transparency and honesty are hallmarks of credibility and reputation. It's the "truth test" of leadership.

Don't hide behind excuses. Refuse to curl into a ball of independence. Reject the urge to fake it until you make it. Be open with the plan, hurdles, mistakes and changes. Involve others to mitigate any of their fears. Include people to surface diverse ways to accomplish the goal. The clearer you are with the strategy—the more authentic you are with yourself and others—the smoother the execution that lies ahead. Truth or dare? Truth always wins. Always.

▶ **PRINCIPLE 3: Focused Foresight**

Perhaps you knew the query was coming: How focused are you on truly completing the strategy? When leaders become distracted by the latest shiny object—SQUIRREL!—it's an unmistakable indicator of one's lack of focus. Sadly, I see a fair amount of it in leadership roles.

Take, for example, the movement towards agile. Just because a *Harvard Business Review* article highlights the plusses of an agile work environment does not mean your team (or organization) ought to immediately implement it. Having "focused foresight" means being able to take in new information while always putting things into perspective. Maybe it's not a good idea to uproot your team, shifting everyone to agile. Change for the sake of change is evidence of a distracted, undisciplined leader. There are plenty of other examples, too. (One-minute management, 360-degree feedback, open office plans and matrix reporting are but a few.)

Staying focused does not mean you refuse ever to change course. Instead, it means you do not distract yourself or the team with superfluous management fads guessing they might help your strategy. (Hint: they often do not.) Have the "focused foresight" to make changes to your strategy or the means by which to achieve it only when necessary.

▶ **PRINCIPLE 4: Load Management**

Your strategy will fail if you are overburdened. Your decision-making prowess will be compromised if you're always on. When the Toronto Raptors won the NBA championship in 2019, much was made of star player Kawhi Leonard's so-called "load management." Leonard was coming off an injury-plagued season in San Antonio prior to being traded to the Raptors, and the Toronto coaching staff wanted to ensure their prized player was ready for a deep playoff run.

The team's strategy was to win the NBA championship. To achieve the goal, management had to carefully calculate how many minutes Leonard ought to play during the regular season, what nights he should play, and what type of recovery methods were required between games. It was decision-making at its finest. It was the command of clarity.

Leonard needed to be rested and healthy for the playoffs. In the end, the strategy and decisions paid off, and the Raptors won their first-ever championship. It's a wonderful example of the importance of load management using clear strategic thinking and decision-making. You will struggle to be successful if you are continually dribbling a basketball. Carve out time in your calendar that permits you to process, think and recover. Your strategy and decision-making ability depend on it. Don't you want to win a championship?

▶ PRINCIPLE 5: Decisive Duty

"The thing that drives me crazy about my boss is his inability to make a decision. It's a joke. I don't even care which way he leans. Just make the freaking call!"

Those were the words from a director during a coaching exchange. Fence-sitting on a decision is one of those loathed leadership traits that often makes it to the top of the least-liked management habit lists. While it is of critical importance to arm yourself with data and evidence before making a decision, waiting too long only causes pain to those you are leading. You have a "decisive duty" to make a judgment promptly. Do not sit too long on a verdict. For if you do, you can be assured people will be talking behind your back about your "paralysis by analysis" tendencies.

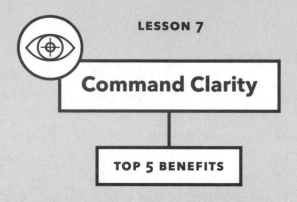

LESSON 7

Command Clarity

TOP 5 BENEFITS

1. Sheep who blindly follow the flock are inferior to the shepherd who clearly sets the strategy.

2. A well-balanced leader without workload issues makes superior decisions.

3. Peers sense your authenticity and will be more likely to buy into your strategy.

4. You set your team up for success by thinking and acting strategically, knowing that your command of clarity is an inspiration to all.

5. The "under-promise/over-deliver" leader is respected and often in line for additional responsibilities or roles.

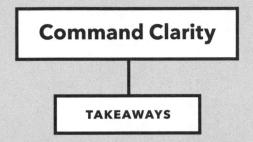

Command Clarity

TAKEAWAYS

Assess your current personal development and growth plan mapped against your organization's strategy. Where are you heading, and should it change based on any newly recognized discrepancies?

Block out time in your calendar to become more strategic with your thinking and to make better decisions. Reinforce how time is linked to the stable mental mood that nurtures clarity.

Reclaim your euthymia: stay focused, act with clarity and add a little cheer to your actions.

Visit www.LeadCareWin.com/extras *for recommended books, essays, videos, quotes, songs, poems and art related to Lesson 7: Command Clarity.*

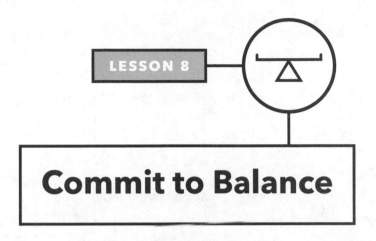

Commit to Balance

I LEFT MY ACADEMIC POST in 2002, at thirty-one, to join a global high-tech company. I became one of about 1,500 employees in my newfound place of employment. The firm earned nearly $250 million in annual revenues at the time. I left the academic world because I wanted to develop my leadership skills, and I will never regret working in the high-tech space between 2002 and 2008, for it was a brilliant learning experience.

After only two weeks in my new role, the founder and CEO of the company announced he was stepping down from active duty to become chairman of the board. The new CEO was hand-picked following a successful 25-year career at IBM as a vice-president of marketing. It was precisely the kind of real-world experience I was looking for. Change was gonna come. A new CEO after a couple of weeks? Bring it on.

I wasn't privy to any of the behind-the-scenes machinations that ensued upon the new CEO's arrival. It wasn't as though I was invited to chats in the C-suite. Interestingly, a mere nine months after his arrival, he announced that we were to be acquired by a high-tech firm based in Paris. Change was gonna come again. Once more, I revelled in the fortuitous real-world experience. Bring it on.

In those nine months, I had ample opportunity to see how the CEO operated. I noticed, as most did, that he sat in his office pretty much all day long. At least when he was in town. It was a small headquarters; the floors creaked, the cavernous stairwells echoed and the aromas of lunch floated through the space. You could always sense when people were about to get up to make tea. Everyone was pretty much on a first-name basis, yet the CEO seemed as though he didn't want anything to do with us.

When he arrived, talk spread rather quickly that one of his first orders of business was to purchase a new desk—a new desk for the office he apparently never planned to leave. To make matters worse, word leaked out that the new desk had a marble top. The desk that had once served the now-chairman was constructed of oak or pine. The new-desk ignominy did not sit well with many employees. Apparently it was easier to sign checks on a marble desktop.

Why would the purchase—or the composition—of a new desk rub some people the wrong way? I believe that the desk symbolized the CEO's unwillingness to leave his office. Maybe that was the way at IBM, where this CEO had spent most of his career. His marooned-like disposition, signing checks on a shiny marble top, irked me greatly. He was a hermit, metaphorically anchored to his riches. It was not the type of inspiring leadership I was hoping to learn from. But in hindsight, he *did* teach me a lesson about leadership.

That new CEO treated his office—and the fancy new desk—like a perch, not a perk. There was an utter imbalance between him and the employees. He used the office as a bunker, a trench, a divide between his title and team members. His behavior symbolized an unwillingness to coach, listen or recognize the employees who would eventually make him millions through the sale to another company. It is the very example, symbolically, emblematically and specifically, that you need to avoid at all costs if you want to become a leader who matters.

Leadership is not to be conducted from a perch. It is a privilege. You must commit to balance. Your ability to be an effective leader depends on it.

The Problem

One of the most successful companies in the modern era was forced to admit it had lost its way with its employees. That company was Microsoft. Once Satya Nadella took over as the company's third-ever CEO in 2014, he quickly went to work, instilling a culture of clarity, empathy, diversity and inclusion, one backed by new leadership habits: listen, coach and recognize.

Nadella promoted Kathleen Hogan to Microsoft's chief people officer and executive vice-president of Human Resources. To say Hogan deftly recognized the various leadership problems that plagued the organization is akin to chronicling how swiftly children burst into the street moments after hearing the sweet sounds of an ice cream truck. The commitment to balance was now in full swing.

One of the first issues Hogan tackled was to rid the organization of the one-hundred-odd leadership competencies and skills that its leaders were expected to live up to. With feedback from the organization, Microsoft whittled the leadership model down to three actions:

· create clarity;
· generate energy; and
· deliver success.

However, Hogan felt leaders needed something simple to remind them of their duty to develop their team. She launched the "model, coach and care" framework across the company. Unsurprisingly, the company used my good friend Michael Bungay Stanier's excellent book *The Coaching Habit* and related training modules to help the cause.

Hogan and Nadella ultimately recognized that Microsoft leaders had become isolated due to the company's culture. The new leadership habits were to listen, coach and recognize good work. In other words, they introduced attributes that grew leader awareness.

The hermit CEO I witnessed firsthand in my new role at the high-tech company worked in isolation, barricaded in a type of ivory tower, never mingling with employees. It felt very imbalanced. There was no awareness on his part. How do you think it affected people's morale, engagement and well-being? For a revenue-generating unit, it can affect all sorts of financial metrics, too. Whatever type of organization you work for, it will definitively affect customer satisfaction somewhere downstream.

Before the ascension of Nadella and Hogan into their new roles, Microsoft was mired in a deep crisis. It was not a coaching organization, nor did it listen to or generally recognize its people. It was an organization of squabbling, uneven, competitive fiefdoms that engaged in wicked infighting. The misguided DNA of a corner office leadership perch was manifesting right across the organization.

Steve Ballmer—Microsoft's CEO between 2000 and 2014—produced a mixed bag of successes during his tenure. On the one hand, he did grow the company's revenues to $78 billion. A particular portion of that was by acquisition and product price increases. The workforce grew to over one hundred thousand as well. That's the good news. The bad news was Microsoft's market capitalization, which plunged over the course of his tenure from $550 billion—when it was the world's most valuable company, in 2000—to below $270 billion near the end of his reign. Employee engagement sagged as well. So too, Microsoft's stock price never crossed $40 throughout Ballmer's tenure, spending much of that time in the teens.

In part, the dramatic drop in market capitalization and employee engagement and the stagnant stock price were due to the omnipresent corner office perch behavior that I am asking you to avoid like the plague. There wasn't a coaching culture at Microsoft. Nobody was genuinely listening to one another. There surely wasn't a leadership environment of recognizing employees.

Siloed thinking was rampant. There was backbiting. Everywhere. Figurative knife fights broke out among employees, inspired by the leadership perching. Management happened by email. Yelling was normal. Decisions occurred behind closed doors. Hierarchical thinking got exacerbated by ignorance, fueled by ego and riddled with wobbly character. It was becoming an unmitigated tragedy. The company painfully but slowly began to slip away.

Windows Vista. The Yahoo! debacle. Zune. Windows phone. Kin phones. The list of decision disasters goes on. Ballmer infamously once said, "There's no chance that the iPhone is going to get any significant market share."[1] Give him credit, Ballmer took chances. But the process—by enabling a metaphorical culture of unbalanced corner office perches—did not foster long-term, customer-centric and employee-friendly vision. It's no wonder Microsoft co-founder and chairman Bill Gates made the CEO switch in 2014.

Enter Nadella and Hogan. They took one sharp look at the firm and knew it had to shift from a bunch of infighting "know-it-alls" to an organization that coached, listened and recognized its members. After all, they were both "Microsofties," having spent the better part of their careers at the company.

Nadella urged the company to become "learn-it-alls" not "know-it-alls." He and Hogan managed to dig Microsoft out of its deep cultural ditch and rebalance the company, which eventually made it back to the top of the world's most-valuable-company list. Its employees are much more engaged, and the company is a leading—some say *the* leading—innovator in the cloud, gaming and artificial intelligence space. So long, Windows 95. Goodbye, Clippy.

The problem presented in this lesson is simple: if you believe leadership happens from behind a desk or by the pressing of buttons on a digital device—without any thought about collaborating with your team, listening to their viewpoints, recognizing their achievements, coaching them to greater heights, tackling diversity issues head-on and continuously being inclusive—you will find yourself staring up at the proverbial skies from a deep hole. It is not the sort of balance a caring leader exudes. Just ask Microsoft during the Ballmer years. Are you listening, Kodak? Are you reading this, BlackBerry?

5 LEADERSHIP QUESTIONS TO ASK YOURSELF

1. Do I make time to coach my team members? (Do I even know how to?)
2. Have I been operating blindly, misunderstanding the distinct meanings of equity, diversity and inclusion?
3. Is my leadership style one that takes employees' circumstances into account when it comes to work arrangements?
4. How often do I recognize my team? Am I using formal and informal ways to do so?
5. Am I worried about team members working remotely, assuming they won't be as productive?

Why Committing to Balance Matters

You may have come across the term "shadow IT." Loosely defined, it's when employees outside of the corporate IT department choose to purchase services or products on their own. Maybe the corporate IT group offers SharePoint as a productivity tool across the organization, but one outlier team decides to buy licenses to Basecamp or Slack with their own budget because they think it's a better overall experience. (They're right, by the way.)

But do you know about "shadow corporate culture?" It's when employees ignore the nonsense of clueless leaders to do whatever it takes to support the customer *and* each other. It happens a fair bit when disconnected leaders lead from perched offices. If you are guilty of such behavior, you will lose. You will lose respect. You will lose the chance to have an engaged team. You will lose out on potential new hires. You will lose the prospect of productivity improvements or innovative ideas. If you are feeling any heat over this, see the signs listed below and look for ones that might be familiar.

Undoubtedly, you will find your team going around you to operate in a way that is more humane, let alone sane. They have pegged you an ineffective leader, and they don't want to go down with the ship. That's when a "shadow corporate culture," or at least a shadow team-operating culture, will come to bear.

I have witnessed "shadow corporate culture" tactics across many organizations and teams, be they corporate, public sector or not-for-profit. It's never a good scene because both sides—the leader and the team—wind up in an adversarial position. Whether you are the team member or the leader, nobody wants it. Both sides would rather tread water in the North Atlantic during a hurricane.

If you discover these rebellious acts of common-sense culture taking place under your nose—because of your penchant to perch— you may wind up humiliated. But that depends on whether you have any empathy left. It may even feel like a coup d'état. However, if you have any empathy at all, you'll know your people were well intended. Most employees only want to do what's right. They want to work on teams that are open, transparent and collaborative. If you are not yet leading a team but are a part of one that has enacted a "shadow corporate culture," have you considered why? Perhaps your direct leader needs some upwards coaching, collaboration or recognition detailing what's really going on behind the scenes.

YOUR "BALANCE" QUOTIENT MAY BE IN PERIL WHEN:

If people want coaching, you think they should join a sport or get a gym membership.

HR keeps sending you memos about diversity and inclusion. You fire back—don't they understand you have a department to run and shouldn't be bothered?

You're busy, so leaving your office is a non-starter. You believe you lead more effectively from behind your desk.

You think a paycheck is sufficient recognition. Not everyone needs a blue ribbon for participation. This is work; it's serious stuff.

You believe remote working is a fad. People need to be in the office to be held accountable and to be trusted. Damn the pandemic!

Go to www.LeadCareWin.com/scorecard *and assess your Commit to Balance score. It will only take a couple of minutes. Then return to the book.*

Ideas for Committing to Balance

Unfortunately, changing your approach is not as simple as stopping yourself from perching in an office or on a desk all day. As the Microsoft example demonstrates, a multifaceted approach is recommended. I suggest six key actions:

▶ DIVERSIFY

▶ INCLUDE

▶ FLEX

▶ RECOGNIZE

▶ COACH

▶ TREK

▶ DIVERSIFY

When I say a leader needs to diversify, I'm not referring to stock or investment portfolios. It's about people. It's about respecting differences and encouraging them, as it concerns your team's structure. To balance is to defend and enact diversity in the workplace.

Diversity in the workforce cannot be thought of as a fad; it has become table stakes. A leader ought to be super conscious of the makeup of their team. When opinions, ideas and habits come from all walks of life, often our judgment becomes less partial. When you open your mind and heart to the world of someone else—when you demonstrate curiosity to have a differentiating mindset a part of your team—the resulting tuition value becomes incalculable. (Recall Lesson 4: Remain Curious.)

Criteria such as race, age, gender, gender identity, marital status, ethnicity, geography, appearance, education, sexual orientation, Indigenous origin, parental status, socioeconomic status, language background and physical abilities are but a few factors that need to be considered in the composition of your team or organization. This not only provides balance but opens up an ocean of uncharted possibilities. If you're a parent, Maya Angelou already has you covered: "It is time for parents to teach young people early on that in diversity, there is beauty, and there is strength."[2]

Accenture is an excellent example. Company executives reviewed their existing diversity practices and acknowledged a change was necessary. While overhauling its hiring processes, the company also set targets. By 2025, for example, Accenture has stated it will achieve a gender-balanced workforce. It is public about its results as well, publishing up-to-date statistics on its website.[3]

As I look back on my career as a leader, I'd argue my diversity track record was hit and miss. Although I pride myself on building gender-balanced, variable-aged teams, I could have done a much better job when it came to diversity. I never explicitly sought a First Nation person or a person with a disability for the team, for example, and I should have. In hindsight, and were I to do it over again today, I'd use the following guidelines as a rubric of sorts:

Assess the current situation.
We are busy. Perhaps overly busy. You may think there is not enough time to take on the diversity file. You are wrong. Your first step, as a team leader, is to assess not only your hiring practices— and the biases that may be present in your recruitment processes— but also the composition of the team itself. Is it homogeneous or ethnically and culturally diverse? Does it model a panoply of thought, gender, background and ideology? That's step one. Assess

how you hire, but also gauge the current composition of your team, and if it is not the vital and creative team it could be, ask why.

Pick a few metrics and focus on them.
Maybe you wish for gender parity. Perhaps you want to emulate the racial makeup of your country or city. Whatever the case, you can't fix it all overnight. Pick a few essential diversity metrics that make sense for your organization or team, and devote yourself to righting the wrong. But don't leave the time frame open-ended. Commit. Take action, just like Accenture.

If you're a CEO or chair of the board, make amends.
I implore you as CEO or chair of the board to set a five-year goal to remedy your people challenges. Can you face up to the fact that your track record is abysmal? It is time to make the composition of your leadership team representative of those who buy or use your products and services, regardless of whether you are for-profit or not. You cannot for a nanosecond expect anyone to fully respect your decision-making if you do not make amends for decades of myopic thinking, leading to biased (mostly white male) leadership and board teams. Honor George Floyd.

▶ **INCLUDE**
If diversity can be thought of as the "what," inclusion is the "how." When you *include* people, it's radically different from addressing your diversity deficiency. Diversity and inclusion do not mean the same thing. When organizations refer to their "D&I" team, I want to scream. People assume D&I is a single issue. It's not.

When you create an inclusive environment—where employees feel valued, safe, respected and motivated to do the right thing—it is a workplace where equanimity reigns. Put differently, there is level-headedness where employees know there is equitable access to opportunities, resources and, yes, leaders. Inclusivity is about equal access, not preferential treatment.

Inclusivity relates to behavior. You aim to be collaborative, opening up your head and heart to the thoughts, viewpoints and opinions of others. (Lesson 1: Be Relatable and Lesson 5: Embrace Change come in handy, too.) That's why there is confusion when the terms "Diversity" and "Inclusion" get lumped together. Being inclusive does not solve your diversity issues. But being more diverse does not mean you have addressed your inclusivity failings either. Try these tactics to become more inclusive:

Help your team members feel that they belong.
This is the quintessence of being inclusive. When your employees can openly discuss how great it is to be part of your team (or not), you have become an inclusive leader. Your team members first need to feel like they belong. Accept their differences. Welcome their ideas. Chat about their backgrounds. Seek to appreciate their viewpoints, if different from yours. Belongingness is not about you; it's about your team member's psychological safety. People need to believe they are safe to be authentic, to collaborate, and to opine.

Ask questions unrelated to work.
I started this chapter with a story about the high-tech company I joined in 2002. A few weeks into my role, my vice-president, Eric

Driscoll, asked me a question. "Dan, you've got a few team members based in cities not named Vancouver. Have you thought about visiting them yet, seeing what's going on in their lives?" Eric provided an invaluable lesson. Get off your perch, but more importantly, reach out and find out what's going on in the lives of the people you support. I ventured off to a few cities in the UK and US to say hello. I will never forget that lesson of asking people questions unrelated to their place of work. These queries are necessary to inclusivity, to creating belongingness and psychological safety.

Create ERGs and ENs.
What's not to like about the creation of employee resource groups (ERGs) and employee networks (ENs) that foster inclusivity? Your organization, be it for-profit, public-sector or not-for-profit, ought to offer access to ERGs and ENs, so employees of differing makeups feel as though they have a community. Perhaps it's an LGBTQ group. Maybe it's a women's group. How about a First Nations/ Indigenous council? Asian/East Indian? The inclusivity list of options is bountiful. The more attention you pay to the unique makeup of your employee population or team, the more likely your team members will feel like they are being heard, and thus included. Again, honor George Floyd.

▶ **FLEX**
When you perform frequent environmental scans of your team members' personal and professional circumstances, you are far likelier to observe items that may be affecting their lives. Those changes might be impacting their well-being. One of those scans

could lead to a change in the way they perform their work duties, out of necessity. Your compassion will likely be the arbiter. The change I am asking you to be on the lookout for can lead to the introduction of a flexible work arrangement. It's time to flex. Out of necessity, the pandemic might even have expedited your thinking on this topic.

A manager once approached me after I delivered a keynote, tears rolling down her face. "What's the matter, and how can I help?" I asked, giving a platonic hug in the process. "Dan, your message resonated with me. I think I'm doing a lot of what you're talking about with my team. But my boss doesn't get it. He doesn't understand me and my personal situation." This poor individual went on to explain how difficult life had become over the past six months with a mother who had entered the throes of dementia. "My director doesn't seem to care that I'm a single parent of two college students, trying to balance work, home and the time required to attend to my mom's needs at her care home. What should I do?"

One of the top five worst moves a leader can make when it comes to leadership perching is to ignore the changing face of where work can be performed. If the role is conducive to remote work—and your team member has proven their worth—why on earth are you not allowing them to either permanently or occasionally adopt a flexible work style? It makes no sense to not be flexible. Millions of workers were forced to work from home during the pandemic. Surely you can consider making this an occasional or permanent fixture to your team members' situation going forward.

Flexible work—defined as permitting employees the flexibility to work when and where they are most effective—is an entire book unto itself. For purposes of becoming someone who does not perch, consider these flexible work tactics:

Assess your team's existing roles.
Is each role conducive to being performed away from an office occasionally or permanently? Why or why not? Document it, and then publish it to the team. It's ideal if you use your team to help you assess, demonstrating the willingness to be collaborative.

Assess your team members.
If you assessed existing roles first, as a next step you could adjudicate each individual team member to determine if their performance warrants the opportunity to employ a flexible work style.

Note: it may not only be performance-related, but it could be situational. For example, if a team member has just welcomed a new baby into their family, it may not be a great idea to be working from home for a while.

Create the conditions for flexible work success.
It would help if you changed your leadership habits. Face-to-face meetings will no longer be the norm—nor will seeing your team member on a daily basis in the building—so be prepared to use tools such as instant messaging, webcams, collaboration software and the phone to create consistent collisions and touchpoints with your team members outside the office. (You may even have already used Zoom.) It's even more critical not to perch yourself

in a virtual office when an employee is no longer beside you 100 percent of the time.

Your team members need to change their habits, too. Help them see why it's so important to be proactive, communicative and collaborative. Actively reaching out to you and others on the team is critical to sustaining networks and relationships when off-site, let alone getting the work done.

▶ **RECOGNIZE**

One of the easiest yet most overlooked ways to help employees realize their value is to recognize their efforts. Planting a tree on a service anniversary or sending a templated thank-you card on a birthday is not the type of recognition that really means anything these days. (Although one should not forget service anniversaries or birthdays.)

To recognize someone is to first understand what type of recognition they prefer. Perhaps they appreciate the public lauding, whether in person or virtually. Maybe they don't. There are team members who do not want to see their name in bright lights. In fact, they'd likely rather be caught with their hand stuck in the vending machine. Their point of view is to be respected. Thus, step one is to determine how your team members prefer to be recognized.

Once that matter is sorted, try a few of these recognition tactics:
· Quick, short, private verbal acknowledgements for completing a task, solving a problem, etc.
· One-on-one walking meeting that lasts no more than five minutes, recognizing the employee's growth.

- Instant message, DM, text, email or phone call recognizing an awesome moment of excellence.
- Coffee, tea or lunch with just the two of you, recognizing a significant milestone, act or feat.
- Gift card or monetary appreciation for going above and beyond the call of duty.
- Community donation: some employees would rather you or the organization donate to a cause.
- Formal award, ideally aligned to the employee's behavior over a period of time and mapped to criteria such as innovation, leadership, customer satisfaction, courage, community, volunteerism, etc.
- Outcome award to recognize that an employee has completed a massive project or has had a huge client win or the like.
- Written card (physical or electronic) formally highlighting a noticeable behavior change.
- Spontaneous applause or kudo calls: if it's a face-to-face setting and the team member wishes for public accolades, spontaneous applause or kudo calls among workers (or other public demonstrations) can be very moving for the team member.

▶ **COACH**

As with the intricacies of a flexible work operating culture, a full analysis of the vital nuances of coaching would take an entire book.

For purposes of preventing you from leadership perching, I'd like you to focus on one singular aspect of coaching: *Do it daily. And listen more than you speak.*

Leadership is a daily habit, a muscle that must be stretched, developed and used continuously. If you are to make certain of never becoming a leader who perches, you must coach your team every single day. Leadership is a daily habit—ergo, so too is coaching.

Coaching has become too complicated. Training provided by other companies and coaching gurus has become too theoretical and boring. Even when the overly complicated coaching skill is learned, people do not translate the new insights into action. You end up providing more and often unnecessary advice rather than listening and asking more questions to support the colleague through a decision, action or project.

Coaching is not intended to be a laborious, time-wasting endeavor. When you take the time each day to provide timely, relevant and constructive coaching feedback to a team member, you have raised their chances of performance improvement.

Start first by listening. Listen some more. And then listen a bit more. Once you've finished listening, try to squeeze out just a little more listening. Only then, when all the listening is done, should you provide some feedback that helps your team member with whatever it is that they've been explaining.

Coaching is a daily habit. It's just like leadership. And it can be done in a matter of minutes, not hours or days.

▶ **TREK**

To trek is full-bore simple: get out of the office, step away from your desk and stop barricading yourself with emails and texts. Reach out to the team members that look up to you as "the leader." Rapport is the crux of leadership. So go on out and build some rapport! Start trekking.

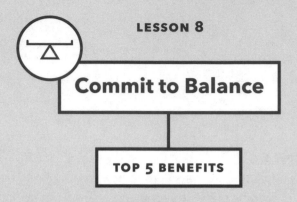

LESSON 8

Commit to Balance

TOP 5 BENEFITS

1. You operate from a position of inclusion, where ideas and opinions are welcomed from all. (And they just may be better than yours.)

2. Peers, leaders and team members view you as an individual who is determined to improve levels of diversity.

3. Your cognitive biases will be lessened—if not eliminated—by your commitment to balance.

4. You will begin to understand what is really going on in the organization by getting out of the office.

5. Lo and behold, you will wind up feeling much better about yourself. (Oxytocin here we come!)

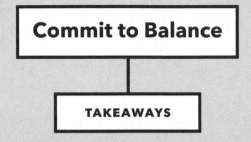

Commit to Balance

TAKEAWAYS

Determine if you are a leader (or individual) who prefers to sit in an office, behind email.

Create the conditions where you will commit to balance. In doing so you will diversify, include, flex, recognize, coach and trek.

Disregard any notion that employees won't create a shadow culture if your style is imbalanced.

Visit www.LeadCareWin.com/extras *for recommended books, essays, videos, quotes, songs, poems and art related to Lesson 8: Commit to Balance.*

Champion Others

IN THE SUMMER OF 2019, at the 128th Canadian Open, in Toronto, Bianca Andreescu had played superbly, earning a place in the championship match against Serena Williams, arguably history's greatest female tennis player. At nineteen years her elder, Williams also happened to be Andreescu's idol.

The first set of the match was underway. The home crowd was ecstatically behind Andreescu. After all, Toronto was her hometown. They were loud, boisterous and hoping for a Canadian win on Canadian soil. If Andreescu won, it would be the first time in fifty years that a Canadian claimed the country's national tennis prize.

Andreescu quickly went up three games to one, dominating Williams in many facets of the match. At the scheduled break before the fifth game, Andreescu took her usual seat beside the umpire to rehydrate and recuperate. Williams did the same. During the interlude, many were admiring Andreescu's pace, fortitude and scorching returns. Overall, Williams appeared to be no match for her on this day.

It was at this point that a deep example of humility and caring emerged. Looking distraught and shaken, Williams indicated to the umpire that, because of an issue with her back, she could not continue. Her coach and therapist confirmed her injury. In tennis parlance, Williams abandoned the match.

While not unprecedented for a championship, it was undoubtedly a shock to everyone in the stadium and those watching on television. The big bowl of popcorn I made went untouched.

Looking somewhat incredulous after the umpire announced the match was over, Andreescu quickly sprung up. She didn't sprint out onto the court to accept congratulations from the adoring yet confused hometown crowd. No, Andreescu dashed over to the now sobbing Williams, gave her a huge hug, and then kneeled at her side as if bowing to the queen of tennis.

"I'm sorry this happened to you," said Andreescu in the middle of the hug. "What's happening?" she asked. Williams spoke of her pain, and Andreescu responded, "Don't even get me started," an empathic comment given her history of injuries.

Andreescu continued, "You know, I've watched you your whole career. You are a fucking beast. Injuries? I've been through so many already. This sucks. It's your back, right? Ha! I know everything about you." After the exchange finished, they both stood up and hugged one another tightly.

About thirty minutes later, as Andreescu was being presented with the trophy, Williams addressed the crowd. "I'm not a crier," she ironically said through the tears. "Thank you guys, I'm sorry I couldn't do it today. Bianca, you're a great sportsperson, woman. And thanks to my team, we'll keep going."

Williams could not hold back the tears. It was as humbling a moment as any champion has demonstrated, let alone one who has garnered twenty-three major tennis titles (the most by any woman or man at the time of this writing).

On that court in 2019, Andreescu and Williams demonstrated a remarkable level of humility, of unpretentiousness. They might have been "beasts" as competitors, but they were also in each other's corner.

Bianca didn't want to win that way. Serena didn't want to lose in that manner. But neither of these extraordinary women made it about herself; they looked past their egos and naturally gave in to a slice of humble pie. They respected one another. They respected the game. They oozed admiration. Ultimately, they were champions for each other.

Humility: it's an incredible, everlasting leadership gift. The lesson is simple for aspiring leaders of self and of others, like you. How good are you at making what you do about others? If I can be honest, there's too much false pride and narcissism going on in leadership circles this day and age.

It's time for leaders to be far more modest and humble, just like Bianca and Serena. Start caring. Be kind. Become the champion of other people.

The Problem

Years ago, in 1999, when I was a director for an academic program at the British Columbia Institute of Technology, I was facilitating an afternoon session with the first-ever cohort. I did something incredibly stupid. I embarrassed a student in front of the entire class. I made the situation about me, at the expense of this unfortunate person. There was no modesty, no humility, only self-centeredness in my actions. I certainly wasn't caring. I most definitely was not championing others. When we're immodest as leaders, it can lead to a damaged reputation, among other problematic outcomes.

The student's name was Calen Slezash. At the time, the class and I were discussing concepts related to collaborative behavior. (Talk about irony!) From my recollection, it was riveting dialogue. As is my usual style, instead of being at the front of the classroom, I was walking around the room, discussing and engaging with the students from all corners of our little agora.

At one point, Calen chimed in and launched into a commentary. I was two meters away from him. I quickly judged his thoughts as irrelevant. "Calen's comment does not make sense at all," I thought to myself.

And, without missing a beat—perhaps looking for a laugh from the rest of the class—I cut him off and said, "Calen, talk to the hand." Standing near him, I raised my hand in front of his face while I said those dreadful words.

Now, we all make mistakes, but the one I made in front of the class at the expense of Calen was outright reprehensible. I made the situation about me, not Calen, the class or the in-flight discussion. It's an incident that still haunts me to this day. I was the champion of no one.

The class continued for another thirty minutes or so, but I could sense how hurtful my actions were to Calen. He slumped back in his chair, face dejected, never contributing again to the afternoon's topic.

Back in my office, towards the end of the afternoon, there stood Calen in the doorway. He called out my arrogance, my utter disrespect for his feelings *and* the way he learns. By the end of that twenty-minute meeting, we were both in tears. I apologized profusely. Thankfully, Calen accepted it. Ultimately Calen helped me understand how hurtful the situation was and what I should have done differently. Calen was a verbal processor, and making oral statements or asking questions out loud was simply part of his learning style. I cut him off at the knees with my arrogance and lack of decorum. I was demonstrating EDD: empathy deficit disorder.

I learned a great deal from that moment because of his willingness to teach me. Yes, Calen's caring taught me a lot about caring.

Twenty years later, I asked Calen if I could tell the story in this book. He immediately obliged and filled me in on how it was such a pivotal moment for him, too: "Funny that what I had learned in the class already (likely from you) is what drove me to take control of my own learning and to speak to you about it afterwards. But most importantly, it was the day that I learned 'how I learn.' I think it stems from taking responsibility to learn on one's own, and then reaching out for answers or clarifications. I have always sensed that that moment has stuck with you. It has with me too, and in a good way."

What if Calen had taken my arrogant behavior up the chain and reported my poor conduct to the dean? That would not have ended well. How did other students view my egotism? Did I rub them the wrong way as well? Had I done it before and not known about it?

We will sail in an ocean of problems if we choose superiority over humility. We will be unable to build trust or a reputation;

make friends; offer counsel or comfort; collaborate with others—the list of related problems is almost infinite. The key is to champion others, not to make it solely about yourself. (And thank you, Calen, for teaching me the importance of it so many years ago.)

FIVE LEADERSHIP QUESTIONS TO ASK YOURSELF

1. Do I treat people fairly, and am I mindful of their intellect, gripes, pay level and growth needs?
2. Do I come to work wearing a Teflon suit, pretending to be someone I'm not?
3. When things go sideways, or an objective gets achieved, am I considerate of other people's feelings?
4. How do I ensure goals get achieved, yet remain attentive to both workplace and societal issues?
5. What's my goal as a leader: self-centeredness or selflessness?

Why Championing Others Matters

If you are currently a CEO of a publicly traded company—or aspire to be one—perhaps the following data point will help. Oleg Petrenko, an assistant professor at Texas Tech University and co-author of the paper *The Case for Humble Expectations: CEO Humility and Market Performance*, discovered that the level of humility a CEO demonstrates can result in up to a 7 percent rise in annual shareholder return.[1] In my view, so long as shareholder return gets treated as an outcome of an engaged workforce—and not the primary goal of the firm itself—there is a lot to like about Petrenko's findings. It literally pays to care about others.

Another research project, led by Amy Y. Ou, confirmed that "when a more humble CEO leads a firm, its top management team is more likely to collaborate, share information, jointly make decisions, and possess a shared vision."[2] In my experience, when leaders and employees operate more communally towards a goal or work more collaboratively on a project, the benefits accrue steadfastly for many parts of the organization. Humility leads to better teamwork, which leads to higher levels of engagement. There's a wonderful trickle-down effect that blankets the organization.

For example, when a Canadian-based Crown corporation became worried about its level of employee engagement and related behaviors in 2015, my colleagues and I were asked to conduct an enterprise-wide culture assessment to see what was working and what wasn't. One illustration: 48 percent of employees considered the leadership structure to be too closed, non-collaborative and uncommunicative. That's half the organization. Fast-forward four years, and after implementing some key recommendations—which included leadership behaviors related to championing others—that same benchmark decreased to roughly 20 percent. Four-fifths of team members then felt their leaders were open, collaborative and communicative. Overall employee engagement also increased, as did customer service satisfaction scores.

Amy Y. Ou and her collaborators also revealed that if modesty becomes part of a CEO's behavior, a lower pay disparity between the CEO and senior leadership team members will result. A humble

CEO knows that outlandish compensation gaps—let alone gender pay gaps—do not demonstrate a caring attitude. That's about as humble as Napoleon's egocentric decision to coronate himself in 1804. Despite Pope Pius VII's alleged agreement to officiate, France's new emperor literally placed the crown on himself at Notre-Dame cathedral, disdaining the pope's traditional role in crowning emperors. Imagine crowning yourself queen or king. Years later, things didn't work out so well for poor old Napoleon after he lost the Battle of Waterloo and was sent to live out his days on the tiny island of St. Helena, a wind-swept, barren rock located in the South Atlantic Ocean.

Ou and her researcher colleagues also found that leaders would "be more likely to adopt an ambidextrous strategic orientation," which itself would be tied to stronger overall performance when demonstrating high levels of humility. My experience with the Crown corporation mentioned above was very similar. Humility opens doors. Caring about others is not a bad thing. After surveying 2,500 millennials across Australia, Brazil, China, Germany, India, the UK and the US, research firm Egon Zehnder discovered that roughly half of all leaders in this age bracket feel humility to be the most desirable characteristic of a leader.[3] In my experience, millennials do not care for the self-centered, emotionally unintelligent type of leader. There is no need for Napoleon in the twenty-first century.

Although the data does not yet exist for Generation Z—the generation younger than millennials, born between 1997 and 2012—I suspect the need for leaders who care more about people is even higher for this group. You need not look very far. (I don't have to look very far at all, as I'm raising three very vocal and crusade-driven Gen Z children, born in 2003, 2005 and 2007 respectively.)

Greta Thunberg's inspiring environmental activism and Varshini Prakash's similar efforts with the Sunrise Movement—as well as the work of Sage Grace Dolan-Sandrino and Sarah Chadwick, co-founders of March for Our Lives, a Gen Z-led political action committee for gun control stemming from the Stoneman Douglas High School shooting in Parkland, Florida—are sublime examples of Gen Z putting everyone ahead of their own egos. This generation seems to champion others (and the planet) with abundance. A research study by Sparks & Honey in 2014 found that 26 percent of sixteen- to-nineteen-year-olds already volunteer regularly, a gaggle of teenagers situated smack in the middle of the Gen Z age bracket.[4]

Back to you, the aspiring leader of self and others. What precisely can you look forward to as a leader if you metaphorically pilot the airplane with much higher doses of care? Research suggests your team will have lower absenteeism,[5] lower attrition[6] and increased team confidence, as well as higher team performance.[7] Unsurprisingly, additional research on the merits of becoming a modest, humble leader indicates employees feel more engaged and trusted and are much less likely to quit.[8] It is a no-brainer. There is much to love about being a caring, humility-based leader who champions others.

Ideas for Championing Others

You are likely a relatively caring human being already. We tend to have a natural disposition to both look out for ourselves—a little bit of self-centeredness—*and* look out for others. Unlike Napoleon's example of deliberately crowning himself emperor, in my experience people exhibit humility every day.

The next question is how often you demonstrate it and to what depth. Your busyness is indeed a culprit. The busier you are—the more packed your calendar is with back-to-back-to-back meetings—the less likely you have time to contemplate how to champion others. It's a dilemma, and it always will be. Demands on your time will always threaten to counter your humility aptitude.

But I've got good news. There are ten useful tactics I've picked up over my career that can assist you further in your quest to champion others. Some of them I've cultivated myself, whereas others I've observed from extraordinary leaders.

▶ BREAK THE MIRROR

To put it bluntly, stop making everything solely about you. In Lesson 2: Play for Meaning, we discussed the notion of whether, when it comes to the concept of purpose and meaning, you're playing for the name on the back of your jersey or the crest on the front. Analogously, are you continually staring in the mirror for individual accolades, or should you break it?

When you "break the mirror," you no longer make everything about you. Your decision-making should begin first and foremost with thinking about the impact your actions will have on others.

When you "break the mirror," you are no longer seeing the world through the veneer of egocentrism.

▶ GET NAKED

While it sounds like a violation that is certain to land you an asterisk on your employee file, getting naked is as natural an act as you'll ever consider on the topic of championing others.

171

First, what are your weaknesses? We all have them. For example, I make up words, am horrible at bookkeeping, don't say "no" enough, write longer emails than may be required, assume people know what I'm thinking and eat far too many Pontefract Cakes, the delicious black licorices originally manufactured in the Yorkshire town of Pontefract, England.

Share your weaknesses with those who matter, be it your team, boss, colleagues or even your family members. Watch them smile at your vulnerability.

Then humbly divulge what you're really good at—you may even want to call them "strengths"—and highlight how those assets make you a better person. "Being humble and sharing your strengths" may sound a bit like "jumbo shrimp"—an oxymoron—but it demonstrates how willing you are to put those strengths of yours on the line to move the team's objectives forward.

▶ **HIRE (AND LET GO OF) PEOPLE SMARTER THAN YOU**

You've made it to a leadership role. Maybe you've been promoted to an even more senior position. Review the team you've inherited. Now, formally assess everyone. Take your time. Call it the "look, listen and learn" tour. Once that's complete, does the team possess the kind of talent that is going to help you achieve your goals? Equally important, is your team smarter than you?

More often than not, three things should occur after the tour is complete:

· You need to hire people who are smarter than you to enhance the team's skill level.

· You need to develop people to reach a level of competence higher than yours, such that the goals get achieved.
· You need to allow people smarter than you to go free, realizing their talents might be better suited elsewhere in the organization.

▶ **SAY, "I DON'T KNOW."**

"I don't know": it's the very definition of humility. It's okay not to know everything, to be stumped, to wonder how you ended up in a leadership position in the first place.

But that's the beauty of saying, "I don't know." When you do so, you're putting yourself in a situation where your team members (or boss) can help you with the unknown.

Just be careful. Overuse the term and you will likely wind up looking incompetent. A proper balance is required.

▶ **PLAY *JEOPARDY!***

As with the television game show where an answer is presented first, why not "play *Jeopardy!*" and ask questions? Questions can surface gaps, and gaps can be thought of as ways to champion the ideas or thoughts of others. Perhaps it's a question to help simplify, or to seek further understanding, or maybe it's a nifty way for you—as the leader—to engage with a team member in a more meaningful way.

When used appropriately, questions can help unleash another form of caring. They can act as catalysts for clarification, something every humble leader ought to employ.

▶ REVERSE MENTORS

There is nothing wrong with mentors or coaches—seeking out assistance is itself a noble act—but all too often the people selected are older than you, chosen for their experience, background or career exploits.

A reverse mentor offers all the goodness of having someone provide you with sage advice, but that person or persons are younger than you.

Reverse mentors help you see through the blind spots of your age and biases—another way to diffuse your immodesty.

Depending on your age, I generally recommend at least one reverse mentor per generation. For example, as a member of Gen X, I have one millennial and one Gen Z reverse mentor. I typically change them out yearly and meet three to four times per year for a beverage, quizzing them on all sorts of topics and my blind spots.

▶ START SKIPPING

I loved skipping as a kid. Perhaps it's why I always find a way in which to meet with team members who were not direct reports but were further down the organization chart. It's one of the first actions I recommend to those I am executive coaching.

There is so much to learn from a skip-level meeting. As you go further down the org chart, you will find additional nuggets of intelligence, ideas and feedback lying in wait.

The benefits are clear. First, you get the truth, cleansed from any upward sanitizing. Second, those skip-level encounters act as another opportunity to demonstrate how much you care about others and that you don't live (or lead) from a white ivory tower (see Lesson 8: Commit to Balance).

▶ **VOLUNTOLD**

"Voluntold" is one of those mash-up words that people generally don't like. But I do, primarily when it's one used to get you and your team volunteering in the community.

When you lead by example in the community, you and your team are donating your time, strengths, skills and intelligence to leave it in a better place, stronger than when you arrived.

Not everyone understands the importance of community volunteering. When we volunteer and help those less fortunate, we are humble servants to society's desperate needs. It is "Championing Others 101."

Given that not everyone may understand or appreciate its significance, you may have to introduce the verb "voluntold."

▶ **RECOGNIZE THEIR PAIN**

The ability to champion others was exhibited with awe-inspiring grace in March 2019 by Jacinda Ardern, prime minister of New Zealand. When an Australian-born white-supremacist terrorist claimed the lives of fifty-one people and injured forty-nine others—all of them at prayer in a Christchurch mosque—she intuitively invoked her knack for empathy, caring and championing others. Ardern genuinely nurtured those affected and recognized their pain, and it showed.

The prime minister's instinct told her to wear a hijab as an expression of solidarity when she met with the families of the victims. She refused to publicly speak the killer's name, exuding deft temperance. When Ardern did provide remarks—to the press or in parliament—her words were as blunt as they were compassionate. She knew the country's citizens were desperate for her to champion the Muslim faith, not petty politics or condescending commentary and toothless talk. Ardern recognized their pain and stood in unison with their loss.

Fast-forward roughly one year to Easter, 2020. It's the middle of the pandemic, and Ardern is thinking about the children of New Zealand. At a press conference, she declared the following: "You'll be pleased to know that we do consider both the tooth fairy and the Easter Bunny to be essential workers." It's another example of how Ardern recognized the pain of others—in this case, many children—and took action to turn fear into relief.

▶ HOLD THE DOOR, LET SOMEONE IN AND SAY GESUNDHEIT!

Manners: I see them effortlessly go by the wayside every day. If you want to be a leader who matters, start first perhaps by remembering the significance of good manners.

Are you leaving the building, an elevator or a meeting room? How about looking behind you to see if anyone is coming before darting off? Maybe there's someone a few feet away as you are exiting—why not pause and hold that door for them?

Are you waiting for the elevator? Why not hold the door and let them go in first? Arrived at the conference lunch queue at the same time as someone else? How about allowing them the chance to fill their plate before you? The options to put yourself before others are endless.

"Gesundheit," the German word for "health," acts as a metaphor for your willingness to say kind things to your colleagues. Whether it's a new haircut, something good that happened on the home front, a published book, or anything in between, say gesundheit and make someone feel better with your demonstrative level of EQ, and of course, your level of caring. (Pro tip: "gesundheit" still can be used if someone sneezes.)

We started the chapter discussing the story of Bianca Andreescu and Serena Williams at the 2019 Canadian Open, so let us end with one final tennis-related account.

In the third round of the men's 2005 Italia Masters tournament in Rome, American Andy Roddick paired up against Spain's Fernando Verdasco. It got to match point in favor of Roddick.

Verdasco hit his second serve. The line judge called the ball out. Match over. The crowd erupted, cheering in unison for Roddick, one of the tournament favorites. As is customary in tennis, Verdasco started walking towards the net to shake hands with Roddick. After all, the match was over.

Roddick didn't walk to the net. Instead, he began arguing with the umpire. Roddick didn't agree with the call by the line judge. "The ball was in," you could hear him say. He motioned to the umpire, pointing to a divot on the clay court surface. That mark clearly showed where the ball had landed: on the line, not beyond. The ball was in bounds. As an aside, there were no computer-aided cameras to assist umpires back in 2005.

The game resumed. Verdasco served again at deuce and won the point. Roddick went on to lose the match, but obviously something else was more important to him. How astonishing.

Roddick didn't make it about Roddick; it was about the game of tennis, the humility of doing what was right for the fans and championing Verdasco.

Roddick 1. Napoleon 0.

For the game and not for personal gain.

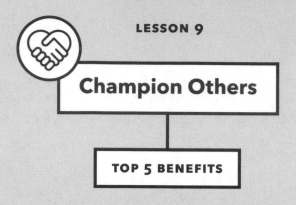

Champion Others

TOP 5 BENEFITS

1. Ego-less camaraderie, the recognition by team members that you've got their backs.

2. Higher-performing, engaged and trusting teams that are willing to go above the call of duty.

3. Respectful workplaces, full of fairly paid people, eager to share and help one another.

4. Community dividends: local neighborhoods and society benefit from your humble altruism.

5. Self-worth: humble leaders die peacefully, knowing they chose to champion others.

Champion Others

TAKEAWAYS

Self-assess for humility and graciousness.

Break the mirror and get naked: two quick wins for leaders of self and others.

Hold the door: no matter your age or tenure, it's your duty to care and help others.

Visit www.LeadCareWin.com/extras *for recommended books, essays, videos, quotes, songs, poems and art related to Lesson 9: Champion Others.*

Coda: Stand By Me

I HAD FLOWN over one and a half million miles in my lifetime, but never to Crescent City.

New Orleans. N'awlins. The Big Easy.

That all changed one spring day in 2019 as I touched down in the land of gumbo and crawfish. I wanted to see if I might have it in me to finish writing the outline for another book. (It turned out to be this book.)

I felt the need to be inspired, so I decided to take in the air of the Mississippi Delta city that gave us Ellen DeGeneres, Truman Capote, Brené Brown, Allen Toussaint, Dr. John, James Burton and of course the great "Satchmo," Louis Armstrong. To breathe in their respective creativity and brilliance was my goal. On one of the nights I was there, I dined at the House of Blues. It's an institution in the Big Easy, a restaurant co-founded by fellow Canadian Dan Aykroyd. Dan and his *Saturday Night Live* co-star John Belushi made up another institution, the Blues Brothers.

After I settled in at my table, a duo began to play, two fellas who were in sync not only sonically but emotionally.

In the first set, the younger of the two musicians took the lead on vocals, simultaneously playing the keys. The older musician (by at least twenty-five years) played percussion and sang background vocals. I was enthralled.

In the second set they switched roles. Near the end of the set, they played Ben E. King's "Stand by Me." It was spellbinding. The notes floated, the harmonies effortlessly dancing on the humid N'awlins air. The older chap introduced the song by saying something simple, yet loving:

"For my wife."

I thought to myself, "How adorable. I wish Denise were here."

A couple of tunes later, they finished their set. They thanked the forty or so people in the restaurant, said their goodbyes, packed up their gear and left the stage.

Before the show ended, I asked the server to place a twenty-dollar bill in a jar that was on the stage. I asked her if the musicians were getting paid for the show. "Not much," she said bluntly. "I think it's about a hundred dollars for the night." Sadly a twenty was all I had.

I drifted off to watch a hockey game on one of the television screens while finishing up my Old Fashioned—mentally revelling in their performance—when, all of a sudden, the older of the two musicians sat down beside me.

"I was making eye contact with you all night," he said energetically. "I just wanted to say hi, and thank you for watching our show."

Somewhat taken aback, I didn't know what to say. I came up with the following: "You two were so fab. Thanks for playing."

"Thanks for playing?" What kind of person says something as puerile as that? He smiled, ignored my inability to say anything intelligent and said, "Well, that's my son. Isn't he great?"

Not only was the son maybe twenty-five years younger, he was at least one hundred pounds heavier as well. There is no way I would have made the connection that it was a father-and-son tandem.

"He sure is," I said warmly.

Then the mic dropped. Not literally, figuratively.

In a deep Louisiana drawl, he said: "It's our first gig since my wife passed. I had to take care of her for a while there. I think we were still pretty good."

I shook his hand and said, "You two were amazing. Love poured through those keys. Your son is probably very proud."

He smiled, thanked me again, and wandered off into a night of shimmering stars somewhere down on the Bayou.

As I walked back to my hotel in the French Quarter, I knew I couldn't return to the book outline just yet. I sat out on the hotel courtyard patio, staring at those shimmering stars, thinking about the lessons I had learned from this man and his son. There may even have been a tear or two that fell into another Old Fashioned.

Each of us possesses a backstory, but we also have various issues we are dealing with at any given moment, just like those two singers. Maybe it's a sibling going through a rough patch. Perhaps one of our offspring is in trouble at school. A parent has been diagnosed with dementia. Maybe you were recently laid off. As the case may be, a pandemic is creating acres of stress in your life.

Maybe you have started a business to follow a dream, and it's a tough go. Maybe a project has gone sideways at work.

Or, not long ago, your spouse passed away.

Life is full of setbacks, bruises and things that seem to have no other purpose than to try to tear us down. How we show up and contribute to each day is one thing. How we both empathize and sympathize with our fellow human beings is another. It is the very essence of leading self *and* leading others. We need to care. We need to give a bother. Leadership matters.

Sometimes we simply don't know what's behind the microphone of those harmonies and melodies. Sometimes we just don't know what's behind an exchange of greetings at work or a sudden absence of one of our colleagues. It's our job as leaders to find out, be respectful and offer a hand as needed. That father-and-son duo was a spellbinding demonstration of two people leading, caring and winning. To my mind, they were the expression of the highest value of what it is to be human: loving, compassionate, kind, forgiving of whatever agency took the life of a wife and mother, and pressing on despite the hardship. They were present, playing to and relating to the audience with meaning, sharing their personal tragedy and story, intentionally or not.

To be a musician, you have to be super curious, constantly curious, or the music becomes stale. You have to be authentic and commit to getting out of the house, or the gigs will never land. Above all, those two men in New Orleans were demonstrating humility as they honored a special woman, playing with and for the love of their craft and their family. Indeed, we should encourage our peers who need help to "stand by me."

The nine lessons in this book are a distillation of my professional life of leading self, leading others and working on the ground with hundreds of different leaders and organizations from all over the world. None of us, even though we may think we are at the top of our game, can deny that we can still all be better leaders, leaders who are more present, caring, curious, clear and relatable. I laid it on the line for you: this book was about you and me and our quality of caring. I was blunt at times. But it's because I care. A lot. About you and the people who surround us and deserve to be cared for. I guess I tried my best through the preceding words to champion *you*.

It was the honor of a lifetime sharing that moment with those men at the House of Blues in N'awlins. I am indebted to them for their inspiration to complete this journey.

In truth, that trip to New Orleans and the exchange that night gave birth to this book. And I am forever grateful.

Full Circle

At the beginning of every Christmas season, my family and I sit down to watch the film *Love Actually*, written and directed by Richard Curtis. It's a tradition we have had since 2003, the year the film appeared in our local cinema. That's also the year our first of three children arrived, so it holds some symbolic sway over our hearts. The opening scene is of people arriving at Heathrow Airport, with a man's voice—that of actor Hugh Grant—asserting the following in a charming English accent: "When the planes hit the Twin Towers, none of the phone calls from people on board were messages of hate or revenge; they were all messages of love. If you look for it, I've got a sneaky feeling you'll find that love actually is all around."

As a leader of self and others, I truly believe love actually *needs to be* all around. Whether or not you love your role at work will inevitably reveal your character. Whether you love interacting with your team, colleagues or various stakeholders will conclusively expose your disposition. Whether you love your organization's strategy, its overarching purpose on this planet, or how the public views it will resolutely inform your leadership.

Love (actually) is needed *more* in the workplace. Your goal? Don't be shy about it.

Having the guts to love yourself, your colleagues, your role, your organization, your career journey is not wrong; it's the mark of out-and-out integrity. I'm not afraid to end this book by insisting that a more caring form of leadership is partially derived from the power of love—specifically, your power *to* love at work.

Love is a word many are afraid to use in their place of work. I believe that's nonsense. In fact, it's regrettable. If you want to be a leader of self and others, you must not be afraid to love at work. If you want to be a leader who matters, adopt a love-based leadership mindset.

After we watched *Love Actually* a couple weeks before Santa's big day in 2019, love actually found a way to be all around me. It was now Christmas Eve, and on this gentle Monday, I was blessed by serendipitous love.

Several years prior, I had come across the story of Dylan Benson, father to Iver. It was an incredibly heartbreaking yet heartwarming tale of love. Iver's mom, Robyn, suffered a terminal brain hemorrhage in late 2013 while pregnant. Dylan—a man of infinite kindness and empathy—lay with his new bride until the doctors indicated it was time to induce labor. There was nothing more they could do. Afterwards they would take Robyn off life support. How horrible a situation it must have been.

When I heard of the family's plight, I wrote about it. I wasn't looking for accolades. I simply wanted the world to know about Dylan's humanity, about how much he cared, about how deeply he loved. Coincidentally, he happened to live in my adopted hometown of Victoria. I felt Dylan needed a boost, even though we had never met.

He came across my article and about a year later reached out to me directly. "The words you wrote were, and still are, one of the nicest things anyone has ever said about me. I was so honored that you took the time to write those words, and they've been helpful to read during difficult times. Thank you. It meant a lot, and it still does."

I replied and said he need not thank me, as his demonstration of courage (and love) was one many ought to look up to. I never did meet him in person.

Fast-forward to Christmas Eve 2019, when I was enjoying a lunchtime pint with my visiting brother-in-law, and in walked a man wearing a fancy Christmas suit bedazzled by brilliantly colored snowflakes. "Oh my, that is something I would wear," I thought to myself.

As he passed our table, I gave a fist bump and said, "Classy suit."

Thirty minutes passed, and then he approached our table again. "You don't happen to be Dan, do you?" said the man in the dashing Christmas polyester.

"Yep, that's me." Despite my similarly Christmas-themed suit, I had no idea who the man might be.

"You're not Dan Pontefract, are you?" he asked.

"Yep, that's still me." And then—as with the two musicians in New Orleans—the mic dropped.

"I'm Dylan Benson."

Immediately, I got up and gave Dylan the warmest of hugs.

"This time of year is really hard," he said. I gave him another hug and promised to meet up with him for a proper pint. We accomplished that in 2020.

But during that moment on Christmas Eve 2019, my heart broke and then warmed again as I thought about Dylan, Iver and the story of their special gal, Robyn.

In summary, love is all around. It's your job to love. Even at work.

Love the inevitable tasks that go sideways.

Love the debates that happen in a meeting.

Love the commute.

Love the coworker who sings in the bathroom.

Love the customer who drives you bonkers.

Love the way your boss never has a difficult conversation.

Love the "reply all" emails that go on for days.

Love the procurement director who overrules your contract.

Love the elevator that is so slow.

Love your colleagues.

Love your organization.

Love your role.

Love yourself.

Love, and I can almost guarantee that you will wind up becoming a *leader who cares.*

As always, thanks for reading.

Love, Dan.
Amor Vincit Omnia

Dylan Benson and Dan Pontefract, Christmas Eve 2019, during a serendipitous moment of love at a pub in Victoria, Canada.

Acknowledgements

I would like to thank Don Loney for his wonderfully astute editing, insight and friendship. Reuniting with Don seven years after *Flat Army* was a magical experience. Thank you, Don.

To the team at Figure 1 Publishing, my hat is tipped to your measured yet impactful guidance. Chris, thanks for sticking with me while providing wonderful mentorship during our whiteboard sessions and pints. Jess, you are an incredible wizard with a ridiculously creative magic wand. To Richard, Lara, Mark, and Peter, my many thanks for your behind-the-scenes assistance on the book's final result and the go-to-market efforts.

I leaned on several people for their feedback and thoughts. I am forever grateful to Michael Bungay Stanier, Liane Davey, Jennifer Smith, Shawn Hunter, Kelsy Trigg, Brian Reid, Alison Lee, Steven Shepard, John Ambrose, Mike Desjardins, Kiran Mohan, Peter Johnston, Steven Hill, Bryan Acker and Mitch Joel for helping me find the right swimming lane. I'm sure the reader thanks you as well. Stephen Lamb for your inspiration. Nilofer Merchant for your honesty. To anyone I've ever worked with (BCIT, Crystal Decisions, Business Objects, SAP, and TELUS) along with the many clients of the Pontefract Group, thank you for teaching me so much about leadership.

To Whitney Johnson, Amy C. Edmondson, Herminia Ibarra and Francesca Gino, thank you so much for reviewing the book and providing the advance book blurbs. I am indebted to your kindness.

To the goats, Claire, Cole and Cate, thanks yet again for allowing Daddio to write another book. It means the world to me that you support my passion. I shall always be in your corner.

And finally, to the love of my life, Denise, I write these words just a few days before our 25th wedding anniversary. Half my life has been spent with you and not a day goes by where I wonder if you know just how damn lucky I feel. I guess it's true, "Everything always works out." Luv ya. xxx

Endnotes

LESSON 1: Be Relatable

1   Customer Guru: Zoom Video Communications Net Promoter Score: https://customer.guru/net-promoter-score/zoom-video-communications.

2   Eric S. Yuan, "A Message to Our Users," *Zoom Blog*, April 1, 2020, https://blog.zoom.us/wordpress/2020/04/01/a-message-to-our-users/.

3   Paul Krugman, "America's Epidemic of Infallibility," *New York Times*, March 20, 2017.

4   Alexander Pope, "An Essay on Criticism: Part 2," Poetry Foundation, https://www.poetryfoundation.org/poems/44897/an-essay-on-criticism-part-2.

5   Katie Marsico, *Madame C.J. Walker* (Ann Arbor, MI: Cherry Lake, 2008), 33.

6   Erik Oster, "KFC Responds to UK Chicken Shortage Scandal with a Timely 'FCK, We're Sorry,'" *Adweek*, February 23, 2018.

7   Francis J. Flynn and Vanessa Lake, "'If You Need Help, Just Ask': Underestimating Compliance with Direct Requests for Help," *Journal of Personality and Social Psychology* 95, no. 1, 128–43.

LESSON 2: Play for Meaning

1   Marc Benioff, "We Need a New Capitalism," *New York Times*, October 14, 2019.

2   In conversation with the author, May 2017.

3   John M. Sweeney, ed., *What I Am Living For: Lessons from the Life and Writings of Thomas Merton* (Notre Dame, IN: Ave Maria Press, 2018), 15.

4 In conversation with the author, June 2019.

5 James Desborough, "Secrets Behind the Making of Supergroup USA for Africa's Charity Hit We Are the World," *Daily Mirror* (London), May 17, 2015.

LESSON 3: Stay Present

1 Timothy Ferriss, *The 4-Hour Workweek* (New York: Crown, 2007), https://fourhourwork week.com/.

2 US Bureau of Labor Statistics, American Time Use Survey, https://www.bls.gov/tus/.

3 "Glassdoor Survey Finds Americans Forfeit Half of Their Earned Vacation / Paid Time Off," May 24, 2017, https://www.glassdoor.com/about-us/glassdoor-survey-finds-americans-forfeit-earned-vacationpaid-time/.

4 Christopher Ingraham, "The Astonishing Human Potential Wasted on Commutes," *Washington Post*, February 25, 2016.

5 "How Japan's Journeymen Suffer Stress on the Daily Commute," Worktech Academy, https://www.worktechacademy.com/japan-suffer-stress-commute/.

6 "The Future of Commuting," Deutsche Bank, March 7, 2019, https://www.db.com/news room_news/2018/the-future-of-commuting-en-11812.htm.

7 "We the Basecamp!," Basecamp website, https://basecamp.com/about.

8 Jason Fried and David Heinemeier Hansson, *It Doesn't Have to Be Crazy at Work* (New York: HarperCollins, 2018), 76.

9 Fried and Heinemeier Hansson, 124.

10 Tobias Lütke (@tobi), Twitter, December 26, 2019, 11:53 a.m., https://twitter.com/tobi/status/1210242184341000192.

11 Paul Petrone, "Stress at Work Report: Who Is Feeling It the Most and How to Combat It," *The Learning Blog*, LinkedIn, April 15, 2019, https://learning.linkedin.com/blog/advancing-your-career/stress-at-work-report--who-is-feeling-it-the-most-and-how-to-com.

12 "Burn-Out an 'Occupational Phenomenon': International Classification of Diseases," World Health Organization, May 28, 2019, https://www.who.int/mental_health/evidence/burn-out/en/.

13 Michael Blanding, "National Health Costs Could Decrease If Managers Reduce Work Stress," *Harvard Business School Working Knowledge*, January 26, 2015, https://hbswk.hbs.edu/item/national-health-costs-could-decrease-if-managers-reduce-work-stress.

14 "Work-Related Stress, Anxiety or Depression Statistics in Great Britain, 2019," Health and Safety Executive (London), October 30, 2019, http://www.hse.gov.uk/statistics/causdis/stress.pdf.

15 Ben Wigert and Sangeeta Agrawal, "Employee Burnout, Part 1: The 5 Main Causes," Gallup, July 12, 2018, https://www.gallup.com/workplace/237059/employee-burnout-part-main-causes.aspx.

16 Marianna Virtanen et al., "Long Working Hours and Sleep Disturbances: The Whitehall II Prospective Cohort Study," *Sleep* 32, no. 6 (June 2009), 737–45.

17 Sara Robinson, "Bring Back the 40-Hour Work Week," *Salon*, March 14, 2012, https://www.salon.com/2012/03/14/bring_back_the_40_hour_work_week/.

18 "Ford Factory Workers Get 40-Hour Week," History, November 13, 2009, https://www.history.com/this-day-in-history/ford-factory-workers-get-40-hour-week.

19 "About Us," Perpetual Guardian website, https://www.perpetualguardian.co.nz/about-us/.

20 "The Perpetual Guardian Four-Day Week Trial," The Four-Day Week White Paper (2019), https://4dayweek.com/access-white-paper.

21 "Case Study 01: Christine Brotherton," The Four-Day Week White Paper (2019), https://4dayweek.com/access-white-paper.

22 "How Much Sleep Do We Really Need?," Sleep Foundation website, https://www.sleepfoundation.org/excessive-sleepiness/support/how-much-sleep-do-we-really-need.

LESSON 4: Remain Curious

1 Francesca Gino, "The Business Case for Curiosity," *Harvard Business Review*, September/October 2018.

2 Jane Sutcliffe, *Walt Disney* (Minneapolis: Lerner, 2009), 45.

3 "Benjamin Franklin," American History Central, https://www.americanhistorycentral.com/entries/benjamin-franklin.

4 Judith McKenna, remarks delivered at the Retail Week 2019 Conference, London, https://live.retail-week.com/.

LESSON 5: Embrace Change

1 "Irving Janis and Groupthink," Wikibooks, https://en.wikibooks.org/wiki/Professionalism/Irving_Janis_and_Groupthink.

2 Karl-Georg Schon, Wit & Wisdom, *Finest Hour* 100 (Autumn 1998).

3 "Change at Work Linked to Employee Stress, Distrust and Intent to Quit, New Survey Finds," American Psychological Association, May 24, 2017, https://www.apa.org/news/press/releases/2017/05/employee-stress.

4 Larry Fink, "A Fundamental Reshaping of Finance," Black-Rock website, https://www.blackrock.com/hk/en/insights/larry-fink-ceo-letter.

5 Dan Pontefract, "Decoding BlackRock Chairman Larry Fink's Letter to CEOs on the Importance of Purpose," *Forbes*, January 26, 2019.

6 Fink, "Fundamental Reshaping."

LESSON 6: Dare to Share

1 National Commission on the BP Deepwater Horizon Oil Spill and Offshore Drilling, *Macondo: The Gulf Oil Disaster: Chief Counsel's Report* (Washington: National Commission on the BP Deepwater Horizon Oil Spill and Offshore Drilling, 2011).

2 Horace Mann, *Life and Works of Horace Mann*, ed. Mary Mann, vol. 3 (Boston, 1868).

LESSON 7: Command Clarity

1 *Merriam-Webster*, s.v. "euthymia (*n.*)," https://www.merriam-webster.com/medical/euthymia.

2 Ryan Holiday and Stephen Hanselman, *The Daily Stoic: 366 Meditations on Wisdom, Perseverance, and the Art of Living* (London: Profile Books, 2016), 23.

3 Scott D. Anthony et al., "2018 Corporate Longevity Forecast: Creative Destruction Is Accelerating," Innosight website, https://www.innosight.com/insight/creative-destruction/.

4 "A Large Share of Small Businesses Are Young Businesses," JPMorgan Chase & Co. website, https://www.jpmorganchase.com/corporate/institute/small-business-longevity.htm.

5 "10 Things You (Probably) Didn't Know about Canadian SMEs," Business Development Bank of Canada website, https://www.bdc.ca/en/articles-tools/business-strategy-planning/manage-business/pages/10-things-didnt-know-canadian-sme.aspx.

6 Joaquim Miranda Sarmento and Luc Renneboog, "Cost Overruns in Public Sector Investment Projects," *Public Works Management & Policy*, 22, no. 2 (2017), 140-64.

7 Matti Siemiatycki, *Cost Overruns on Infrastructure Projects: Patterns, Causes, and Cures* (Toronto: Institute on Municipal Finance and Governance,

2015), https://munkschool
.utoronto.ca/imfg/uploads/334/
imfg_perspectives_no11_cost
overruns_matti_siemiatycki.pdf.

8 David Crouch, "The Swedish
15-Year-Old Who's Cutting
Class to Fight the Climate
Crisis," *Guardian* (Manchester),
September 1, 2018.

9 "Greta Thunberg Quotes: 10
Famous Lines from Teen Activist," *Newsround*, BBC, September 25, 2019, https://www.bbc
.co.uk/newsround/49812183.

10 Robin Pomeroy, "This Is What
Greta Thunberg Just Told
Davos," World Economic Forum
website, January 21, 2020,
https://www.weforum.org/
agenda/2020/01/greta-
thunberg-davos-message-
climate-change/.

11 "Greta Thunberg Quotes."

12 "Greta Thunberg Quotes."

13 Joann Muller, "Davos 2016:
GM Boss Sees a Revolution in
Personal Mobility," *Forbes*,
January 18, 2016.

14 "GM CEO Mary Barra on the
Need for Passion," Duke University—The Fuqua School of
Business channel, YouTube,
posted December 19, 2018,
https://www.youtube.com/
watch?v=7W4OLcg59ys.

LESSON 8: Commit to Balance

1 David Lieberman, "CEO Forum:
Microsoft's Ballmer Having
a 'Great Time,'" *USA Today*,
April 29, 2007.

2 Maya Angelou, *Rainbow in
the Cloud* (New York: Random
House, 2014), 6.

3 "Creating a Culture of
Equality in the Workplace,"
Accenture website, https://
www.accenture.com/us-en/
about/inclusion-diversity/
gender-equality.

LESSON 9: Champion Others

1 Staci Semrad, "Professor's
Research Shows Humble CEOs
More Poised for Success," *Rawls
College News,* June 18, 2019,
https://www.depts.ttu.edu/
rawlsbusiness/news/posts/
2019/06/rawls-professors-
research-shows-humble-ceos-
more-poised-for-success.php.

2 Amy Y. Ou, David A. Waldman
and Suzanne J. Peterson, "Do
Humble CEOs Matter?: An
Examination of CEO Humility
and Firm Outcomes," *Journal of
Management* 44, no. 3 (2018),
1147-73.

3 "Leaders & Daughters 2019
Global Survey," Egon
Zehnder website, https://
www.egonzehnder.com/
leaders-and-daughters/
explore-the-data.

4 "Generation Z: Marketing's Next Big Audience (Infographic)," *Marketo Marketing Blog*, August 2014, https://blog.marketo.com/content/uploads/2014/08/Generation-Z-Marketings-Next-Big-Audience.png.

5 In-Sue Oh et al., "Are Dishonest Extraverts More Harmful than Dishonest Introverts?," *Applied Psychology* 60, no. 3 (2011), 496-516.

6 Bradley P. Owens, Michael D. Johnson and Terence R. Mitchell, "Expressed Humility in Organizations: Implications for Performance, Teams, and Leadership," *Organization Science* 24, no. 5 (2013), 1517-38.

7 Annette Towler, "Team-Efficacy and Team Effectiveness: A Primer for Management Practitioners," CQ Net website, March 31, 2019, https://www.ckju.net/en/dossier/team-efficacy-and-team-effectiveness-primer-management-practitioners/32477.

8 Rob Nielsen, Jennifer A. Marrone and Holly S. Slay, "A New Look at Humility: Exploring the Humility Concept and Its Role in Socialized Charismatic Leadership," *Journal of Leadership & Organizational Studies* 17, no. 1 (2010), 33-43.

About the Author

DAN PONTEFRACT is the founder and CEO of the Pontefract Group, a firm that improves the state of leadership and organizational culture. His goal is to go out of business from a lack of clients who no longer require any assistance.

He is the best-selling author of three books: *Open to Think*, *The Purpose Effect* and *Flat Army*. Dan is a renowned speaker and has been asked to present at four different TED events. He also writes for *Forbes* and *Harvard Business Review*. Dan is an adjunct professor at the University of Victoria Gustavson School of Business and has garnered more than twenty industry awards over his career. His favorite was "Dad of the Year" in 2013, although nepotism was in play.

His third book, *Open to Think*, was the 2019 getAbstract International Book of the Year winner, and it also received a 2019 Axiom Business Book Award in the Leadership category.

Previously as chief envisioner and chief learning officer at TELUS—a Canadian telecommunications company with revenues of over $14 billion and fifty thousand global employees—he launched the Transformation Office, the TELUS MBA, and the TELUS Leadership Philosophy, all award-winning initiatives that dramatically helped to increase the company's employee engagement to record levels of nearly 90 percent. Prior to TELUS, he held senior roles at SAP, Business Objects and the British Columbia Institute of Technology.

Dan's personal declaration of purpose guides much of his thinking: we're not here to see through each other; we're here to see each other through.

Dan and his wife, Denise, have three children and live in Victoria, Canada. If you ever find yourself in Victoria, you'll likely find Dan cycling in search of a locally brewed IPA beer. He may even buy you one.

You can reach Dan on Twitter @dpontefract, Instagram @dan.pontefract, Facebook @danpontefractauthor, LinkedIn @dan.pontefract or on his website at www.danpontefract.com.

Did you know? *Lead. Care. Win.: How to Become a Leader Who Matters* has an accompanying set of online courses. Visit www.leadcarewin.com for details on how to enroll.

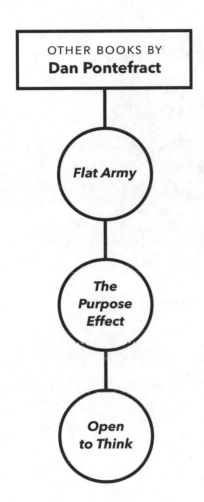

OTHER BOOKS BY
Dan Pontefract

Flat Army

The Purpose Effect

Open to Think

FLAT ARMY:
Creating a Connected and Engaged Organization

"Superb." TOM PETERS

Arms you with powerful tools for overcoming resistance to change and creating a culture of collaboration, engagement, and employee empowerment.

AVAILABLE IN PAPERBACK, EBOOK AND AUDIO BOOK